# Dublin

**A guide to recent architecture**

...

# Dublin

**Angela Brady and Robin Mallalieu**
**Photographs by Keith Collie**

**A guide to recent architecture**

● ● ● **ellipsis KÖNEMANN**

• • •

CREATED, EDITED AND DESIGNED BY
Ellipsis London Limited
55 Charlotte Road London EC2A 3QT
E MAIL ...@ellipsis.co.uk
WWW http://www.ellipsis.co.uk
PUBLISHED IN THE UK AND AFRICA BY
Ellipsis London Limited
SERIES EDITOR Tom Neville
EDITOR Annie Bridges
SERIES DESIGN Jonathan Moberly
LAYOUT Pauline Harrison

COPYRIGHT © 1997 Könemann
Verlagsgesellschaft mbH
Bonner Str. 126, D-50968 Köln
PRODUCTION MANAGER Detlev Schaper
PRINTING AND BINDING Sing Cheong
Printing Ltd
Printed in Hong Kong

ISBN 3 89508 636 3 (Könemann)
ISBN 1 899858 30 X (Ellipsis)

# Contents

# Introduction

The last few years have been a period of unprecedented economic growth in Ireland, fuelled by prodigious European Union grants and the rapid evolution of an agricultural economy into one based around tourism and new 'high-tech' industries. The 'swinging nineties' have seen the international image of Ireland and the Irish reach a comparable zenith, with the 'badge' of emerald green and the shamrock conjuring images of 'old world' charm and the 'craic' in every corner of the globe. But behind this emerald smokescreen lies an energetic, youthful society in a rush to modernise after years in the economic doldrums. Ireland's impressive history of achievement and influence in many fields, particularly music and literature, belies the country's small size – although in addition to its resident population of only 3.5 million it has a 'diaspora' (to use the word popularised by the Irish president Mary Robinson) many times that number spread around the world.

The building fabric of Dublin, as the capital city, has inevitably been greatly affected by this latest economic boom. The common image of Dublin is formed by the Georgian architecture created during the eighteenth century as it rose to be the second city of the British Empire. With the Act of Union in 1800 Dublin entered a period of slow economic decline, during which time a lack of resources helped to preserve the Georgian city. And it survived almost intact throughout the 'Troubles' and the civil war surrounding the formation of the Irish state in 1922, until the economic boom of the 1960s. During this headlong rush towards modernity the city's historic fabric was seen by many as an unwanted reminder of the imperial past, and was plundered mercilessly by property developers and an equally rapacious Corporation. Their crimes against the city included road-building proposals of an insane magnitude which blighted whole areas of the city centre for decades. The story of this dark night in Dublin's history is comprehensively covered by the books of Frank McDonald, the architectural correspondent of the *Irish Times*, most notably *The Destruction of Dublin* and *Saving the City*.

One unfortunate consequence of this period was the suburbanisation of the city and the depopulation of its centre. Dublin became split between the north and south sides of the River Liffey, with the more affluent middle classes moving south into the expanding suburbs of County Dublin, and the poor to massive high-rise social housing developments to the north. On the south side, the area around Merrion Square and St Stephen's Green became the shopping and business district and home to major new commercial developments, while the north side became a wasteland of blight and decay.

Although the 1960s produced a number of distinguished modern buildings, particularly from the practices of Scott Tallon Walker and Stephenson Gibney, the general scene – in common with much of Europe at the time – was one of regrettable demolitions and bland commercial blocks, constructed without regard to site or context. On the few occasions when surroundings were acknowledged, the result was more often than not a dreary and gutless pastiche of the Georgian house.

The most sophisticated architecture of the period was created by the office of Scott Tallon Walker Architects, founded by Michael Scott, Ireland's first modern architect and for many years, until his retirement in 1975, the dominant personality on the Irish scene. The practice recognised the classicism inherent in the work of Mies van der Rohe and applied it to the Georgian city, producing buildings which combined a modern spirit with contextual empathy. The Bank of Ireland Headquarters in Baggot Street and, on a smaller scale, the Lisney Building at 24 St Stephen's Green, are typical examples.

Dublin: a guide to recent architecture

The boom of the 1960s was followed by another slow economic decline, reaching a catastrophic nadir during the 1980s in a depression during which construction virtually ground to a halt. Many Dublin architects, particularly the younger ones, had little alternative but to find work abroad, mostly in the UK and America, with the opportunity to return only recently becoming viable.

But at the same time that construction in Dublin was drying up, in Europe there was growing reaction against a modern architecture that was heedless of context and scornful of a city's historic fabric. The work of European figures such as the Krier brothers and Aldo Rossi began to show a new way for cities to develop, acknowledging the importance of historical continuity. In tandem with this approach, the disaster of much modern planning prompted a growing interest in the issue of townscape and true urban design, a cause championed for many years by the *Architectural Review*. An influential edition devoted to Dublin, published in November 1974, discussed how this brand of urbanism could begin to repair what was by then a shattered city.

It is something of a cliché to suggest that architecture benefits from periods of enforced contemplation during an economic depression – although architects suffering work shortages at the time are not likely to agree – but a great deal of the success of recent work in Dublin can be traced back to theoretical work carried out during the recession of the 1980s. This guidebook covers buildings constructed from the middle of that decade to the present day, a period when the lessons of the 1960s' boom have been able to inform the more recent work. Particularly influential was a small group of architects centred around the School of Architecture at University College Dublin. Faced with the disintegration of their once great city and armed with the lessons of European rationalism, the group produced a series of paper projects such as the 'Dublin City Quays' of 1986 and 'The Modern Street' of 1991. These projects illustrated a modern architecture sympathetic to the historic city and tackled important issues such as the repopulation of the city centre, a move away from car-fixated planning, and the role of monuments within the urban grain. Of equal importance was experience gained from working outside the country. A number of the group passed through the office of James Stirling in London, where Stirling's own flirtation with post-modernism grew out of a similar dissatisfaction with the restrictions of modernism. Running hand in hand with this strand of thought, although to have less lasting impact, was a search for a distinctively Irish regionalist style, again reflecting European trends of the time. In 1987, Niall McCullough and Valerie Mulvin, members of the group, published *A Lost Tradition – the Nature of Architecture in Ireland*, followed by *Dublin – An Urban History* in 1989, both historical explorations of the Irish characteristic in architecture and influential in supporting the first faltering steps then being made towards a modern classicism. By the time construction in Ireland began to increase in the early 1990s, these ideas had filtered down through the profession, even as far as some of the big commercial practices, and a new, modern Irish urbanism had evolved. The UCD group themselves evolved into Group 91 and embarked on the major Temple Bar reconstruction, the figurehead project in the city.

Dublin is a small city of some one million people, with only about 160 architectural practices registered with the RIAI, the country's professional institute (the fact that all the work included in this guidebook is drawn from a small pool of architects is a reflection of this). It is also geographically remote, a theme developed in a recent architectural exhibition at the Pompidou Centre in Paris entitled 'Building on the Edge of Europe'.

**Dublin: a guide to recent architecture**

Nevertheless, Dublin is one of the great European cities containing major neo-classical monuments. As a capital city it has, of course, its full complement of national institutions, yet it is on a scale which encourages exploration by foot. The walk from Pearse Station, through Trinity College, Temple Bar and Dublin Castle is an urban journey of unsurpassable interest and variety through the heart of the modern city – and one relatively free of traffic. Part of this variety is created by the acceptance of modern architecture within the city's historic core. There are, however, no buildings by leading foreign architects, nor have any architects of international significance emerged from Ireland itself in recent years. Dublin has also escaped the majority of recent stylistic trends, with post-modernism making only a passing appearance and deconstruction not yet figuring at all. There are, instead, a growing number of skilful and forward-looking architects who, despite the dead-end of regional classicism, are moving towards a definable, contemporary Irish quality, evident in the materiality of recent work by Gilroy McMahon and Shane O'Toole and the continuing formal preoccupations of de Blacam and Meagher.

We are, ourselves, practising architects, working in both the UK and Ireland, and so are all too familiar with the battlefields of contemporary practice. Creating architecture of quality is supremely difficult, requiring not only design skill and understanding but also endless perseverance and a dogged determination not to waver before the myriad compromises and competing interests brought to bear over the life of a project. To try to create a clearly contemporary architecture in a world still suspicious of, and hostile towards, modern architecture simply compounds the problem. Nearly all the buildings we have included have achieved some measure of success in this battlefield, and a few have transcended the process. The task is immeasurably assisted by a sympathetic and supportive client – Temple Bar Properties and Trinity College are but two of the largest and most influential who should be decorated for their repeated patronage of modern design.

The book inevitably reflects our own preoccupations and interests. In particular we have tried to view each building both on its own terms and in the context of the city fabric and the contribution it makes to the rebuilding and enriching of the public realm. For us this is the acid test of building in the city, and the issue of most importance to current urban architecture.

ACKNOWLEDGEMENTS

Thank you: to all the architects who have supplied material and information and found the time to organise site visits and talk to us about their work; to the owners who were so helpful in allowing access to their buildings; to all the architectural magazines whose articles have been invaluable in preparing these comments, in particular the *Irish Architect*; to Paul Kearney and Maria Kiernan for their generous support, hospitality and advice; to Rita Mallalieu for providing the lay person's point of view; to Tom Neville for allowing us the opportunity to indulge in all architects' favourite pastime – sounding off about other architects' work; to Keith Collie for the photography; and to the patience of Jessica Mallalieu, who has now been dragged around more buildings than any three-year-old deserves.

AB and RM, October 1996

Dublin: a guide to recent architecture

# Using this book

Dublin has a small city centre and expansive suburbs to the north, south and west. The edges of the central area are defined by the line of the Royal Canal to the north and the Grand Canal to the south. This guide is divided on this basis, with the suburbs defined as North, South and West Dublin and the city centre divided by the River Liffey into North and South City sections. Within the central area three particular and well-defined areas of extensive new building are picked out: Temple Bar, Trinity College and The Quays.

The centre of Dublin is tightly packed. Getting around is far easier by foot than by public transport, the variety of the streetscape being in any case one of the city's great joys. Buildings marked as 'BUS/TRAIN City Centre' are best reached on foot. The DART (Dublin Area Rapid Transport) is the only rail link and runs around the edge of Dublin Bay linking the coastal suburbs north and south, and only clipping the city centre on its eastern side. The DART follows a picturesque route and is well worth taking for the views alone. Getting around elsewhere is by bus; the service is neither better nor worse than that of most cities.

Transport in Dublin is dominated by the private car and the consequent congestion also affects the bus system. Most buses go from Busaras, the central bus station at Custom House Quay – which is also one of the city's finest modern buildings (by Michael Scott, completed in 1950).

The best street map is the *Dublin City and District Street Guide* published by the Ordnance Survey of Ireland, but it is unwieldy to carry around. Bartholomew publish a neatly folded *Handy Map of Dublin* which is less detailed but nevertheless adequate and rather more portable. For further architectural information, the Royal Institute of the Architects of Ireland publishes the RIAI *Map Guide to the Architecture of Dublin City*, available at its bookshop at 8 Merrion Square, Dublin 2.

**Dublin: a guide to recent architecture**

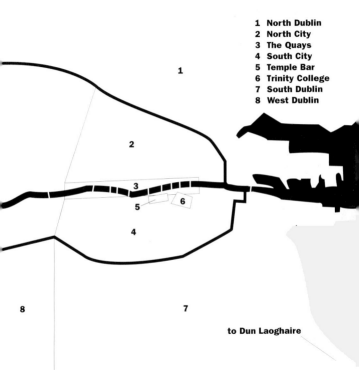

1 North Dublin
2 North City
3 The Quays
4 South City
5 Temple Bar
6 Trinity College
7 South Dublin
8 West Dublin

to Dun Laoghaire

# North Dublin

# Car Park, Dublin Airport

The multi-storey car park presents architects with one of the most problematic of building types, since the function offers little or no content around which the architecture can be based. The usual solution is to resort to fancy dress and pretend that it is not a car park at all, but rather a warehouse or even a theatre (see St Stephen's Green Shopping Centre, page 120). The principal success of this new car park lies in the fact that it is honest about what it is, yet manages to be stylish and attractive. But it is still arguably fancy dress – in this case a sharp International Style suit – though the presence of the original terminal building (a genuine 1937 classic by Desmond Fitzgerald) lends context to the choice.

The car-park complex forms a low-rise 50-metre-wide and 900-metre-circumference ring around the central surface-parking area, absorbing the chapel and other existing buildings into its masterplan. The complex provides parking for 6000 cars and has been carefully planned to leave the minimum distance between car and terminal building. The palette is white-painted reinforced-concrete frame and steel cladding systems to the upper floors, with glass-block details, and a barrel-vaulted arcade signalling the terminal entrance. The best bit is the exit building, which is a summary of the forms and materials used elsewhere spiced with eye-catching lighting and 'super graphics'.

ADDRESS Dublin Airport
CLIENT Aer Rianta
STRUCTURAL ENGINEER Clifton Scannell Emerson Associates
COST IR£10 million
BUS Dublin Airport shuttle from central bus station (Busaras)
ACCESS open

**North Dublin**

**Noel Dowley Architects 1991**

**Noel Dowley Architects 1991**

# The Irish Energy Centre

The Irish Energy Centre is an EC-funded organisation which encourages and advises on the efficient use of energy. The new headquarters of such an organisation is obviously expected to illustrate the principles of low-energy, low-impact design.

The new building is a simple office barn with a narrow two-storey plan, central atrium with glass roof, and open-plan office space. A parallel strip of accommodation houses the service and back-up spaces. Blockwork cross-walls support timber trusses and heavy concrete floors and the infill end elevations are expressed as timber-clad lightweight elements. The central atrium provides a focus for circulation within the centre.

The building is orientated north–south to maximise sun and light, and the heavy construction is highly insulated to act as a thermal store. The narrow plan and large opening windows encourage daylight penetration and natural cross-ventilation. Internally the white painted structure encourages light reflectance.

The centre is a neat and economical illustration of the effectiveness of simple design principles that not only save energy, but also make for an attractive humane environment.

**North Dublin**

ADDRESS Forbairt Campus, Glasnevin, Dublin 9
CLIENT Foras/Forbairt
STRUCTURAL ENGINEER Ove Arup and Partners
COST IR£500,000
BUS 13, 19, 34
ACCESS none

**Energy Research Group, School of Architecture UCD 1996**

**Energy Research Group, School of Architecture UCD 1996**

# Dublin City University

The Dublin City University has grown out of the former National Institute of Higher Education and is the second of Dublin's major tertiary-level educational establishments to be based on a new out-of-town campus – UCD at Bellfield being the other. Arthur Gibney and Partners first became involved in the late 1980s with an extension to the original Albert College and Henry Grattan Building, which led to the development of a masterplan for the expansion of the entire campus into a fully fledged university. Gibney has been responsible for almost all the buildings so far and this has allowed consistency of detailing and materials.

Entry to the site from Collins Avenue gives a view of the rear of the buildings via a pedestrian route from the car park to the main east–west spine, with the original Henry Grattan extension to the right. This building contains a library and offices arranged on either side of a glazed street, which presents a fully glazed gable end to the central spine. The original plan for the university was for a megastructure of closely spaced blocks connected by a series of glazed malls, of which the Grattan extension was to be the first phase. The plan was influenced by Scandinavian architecture, in particular Henning Larsen's Trondheim University. This proved to be a false dawn, however, as the glazed malls failed to attract funding since they were not considered 'educational space'. (Des McMahon's Bolton Street extension was to run into similar problems, see page 70.)

The megastructure was therefore abandoned in 1991 and a more conventional masterplan drawn up, based on a formal linear spine along which individual buildings are arranged. To the south are the social buildings – a sports centre, social centre, chaplaincy and halls of residence. To the north, double banked, are the teaching buildings with arcades at ground-floor level. In addition, the courtyards of the earlier college have

North Dublin

**Arthur Gibney and Partners 1991–**

**Arthur Gibney and Partners 1991–**

been reinforced with new buildings and extensions. The central mall is tree-lined with freestanding pavilions containing shops and a bank.

The campus has very much the feeling of a 'masterplan at work' – uniform materials; a consistent three-storey height; arcading at ground level; a straight, easily extendible spine with 'special' buildings used as incidences of variety; and themed detailing such as the blue-brick stripes to the courtyards behind the main mall. These are economical buildings, often constructed with private-sector funding and therefore expected to be lean and cost-efficient. Funding problems are not the only thing the campus shares with the work of Gilroy McMahon – despite the abandonment of the original masterplan, the influence of Scandinavian modernism is still clearly evident in the soft brown brick and coloured metal window frames, often with a horizontal emphasis. This is a gentle modernism which makes up for a lack of immediate spatial and architectural interest by offering rational planning enlivened with subtle details such as the recessed brick panels and hierarchies of opening size and position which describe the buildings' use and the circulation pattern. Internally, glazed courtyards and rooflights keep the buildings efficient and largely naturally ventilated, ensuring a high degree of user comfort.

Various buildings are positioned to draw attention to themselves. Adjacent to the main entrance route, the circular Larkin Theatre occupies a pivotal position. This is the university's main lecture theatre with a capacity of 400. The simple plan consists of a circular drum constructed as a brick diaphragm wall containing the auditorium, with a brick arcade wrapping round to signal the entrance. With great economy of means, most of the principal architectural themes for the whole campus are summarised and introduced – the brick construction, the square openings within repeated bays, the recessed brick panels and the arcade.

**Arthur Gibney and Partners 1991–**

North Dublin

**Arthur Gibney and Partners 1991–**

Opposite the theatre on the far side of the mall is the chaplaincy, a multi-denominational building with spaces for group and individual worship. The building is the hinge between the original courtyard of the earlier institute and the new mall, the projecting drum and octagon making the transition. Behind the chaplaincy is the R + D Building, which again uses its form to mould the external space, simultaneously completing the original courtyard space and making the transition to the main mall by means of a deft angling of its stair tower. The creation of external space is these buildings' most important role and they modestly sacrifice their own identities to the greater whole.

The consistency of Gibney's work is reflected in the firm's first building for the university, which indicates that the language of the campus was fully formed from the start. Located behind the R + D Building, the extension to Albert College is in many ways the best architecture here. It shares the same vocabulary as the later buildings, but has a more generous solidity to the details. For instance, the incised line defining the bay widths is a full brick recess rather than a vertical mastic joint; the elevations are made entirely of brick without the precast stone coping detail of the later work; and the windows have a horizontal emphasis, a more satisfactory proportion than the later square openings. Its two-storey arcade order is subtly suggested by a minimal recessed window and brick spandrel panel with an expressed lintel above. Many of the differences can no doubt be explained by budget constraints, but looking at this building and the promise inherent in the glazed mall of the Henry Grattan extension, one wonders whether the baby was not washed away with the bath water when the original masterplan was rejected.

The plus side of the new masterplan is the central mall which Gibney has begun to landscape with simple areas of grass, water and paving with

**Arthur Gibney and Partners 1991–**

**Arthur Gibney and Partners 1991–**

long avenues of trees along the edges. The mirror glass and steel pavilions of the shops and bank act as a counterpoint to the brick solidity around. The modesty of the buildings was to be reflected in the landscape design, which should have ensured compatibility and a long life whatever the vagaries of fashion. But the university has recently commissioned new architects to redesign the external space, and current layouts show a trendy, frenetic scheme totally at odds with the architecture. One might have expected that landscape design, by its very nature, would be free from the ephemeral spirit of fashion. The only successful outcome will be if architecture and landscape speak the same language and unify the space.

**North Dublin**

ADDRESS Dublin City University, Collins Avenue, Glasnevin, Dublin 9
CLIENT Dublin City University (Department of Education)
STRUCTURAL ENGINEER Ove Arup and Partners
BUS 11, 11A, 11B, 13, 19A, 36, 36A from city centre and 103 peripheral
ACCESS campus: open; various buildings: by appointment only

**Arthur Gibney and Partners 1991–**

**Arthur Gibney and Partners 1991–**

# GAA Stadium

Croke Park Stadium is the home of Ireland's native sports – Gaelic football and hurling – and is run by the fiercely chauvinist Gaelic Athletics Association. The sports remain hugely popular – the All Ireland Final bring the whole country to a standstill every year and Croke Park has been host to crowds of over 110,000.

Recent changes in stadium safety standards following the Hillsborough disaster in 1989, coupled with the ambition of the GAA to provide a world-class home for its sports, have led to the development of a masterplan to provide a wholly modern 80,000-seat stadium. Phase 1, named the Cusack Stand and representing approximately one third of the total scheme, has now been completed.

Much of the drama of the stand – and it is hugely dramatic – is provided by its inner-city location, with the megastructure towering over its two-storey terraced neighbours. The GAA resisted the temptation to move to an out-of-town location, where problems of access, parking and noise limitation would have been easier to overcome. This worthy decision to remain means that the new building is imbued with the tradition, history and spirit of one hundred years of continuous occupation and at the same time provides the future life of the inner city with a much-needed vote of confidence. Des McMahon is conscious of the need for monuments within the urban fabric and of the importance of scale as a constructive urban design tool – a tool too often overlooked by planners obsessed with being 'in keeping' and 'contextual'.

From outside the ground, the building form is articulated with layers to give a base, middle and top. The completed stadium will eventually be capable of evacuating 80,000 people in eight minutes, so the principal feature of the base is a series of stairs and ramps for this purpose. The spreading out of the concrete stairs at ground level roots the building to

North Dublin

**Gilroy McMahon Architects 1995**

the ground, with the taller ramp and stair structures growing up from the base in immaculate concrete enlivened with ceramic strips.

The first of three horizontal concourses behind the raked seating marks the beginning of the 'middle', where the concrete frame becomes almost organic in articulation as it rises to support the seating in five separate tiers cantilevering forward towards the pitch. Beneath the sheltering frame sits the secondary accommodation of hospitality suites, bars and restaurants, housed within a dark blue panelled stripe around the building's midriff. The seating overhead is neatly expressed with corrugations of concrete beams between the main framing, giving the creature an underbelly.

The 'top' section is literally the crowning glory as the construction changes to a steel suspension structure supporting the dramatic cantilevered canopy which shelters the seating below. From the pitch side, the ranks of shallow vaults, alternating between strips of rooflights that indicate the main truss positions, are a 'look, no hands' epic. From outside, the filigree of grey-painted struts, posts and hangers combines with the concrete frame from which it springs to create an eloquent and dramatic composition as the building meets the sky. The stand is already one of the most distinctive landmarks in north Dublin, a role which will only increase as the further phases are completed.

ADDRESS Croke Park, Jones's Road, Dublin 3
CLIENT Cumann Luthchleas Gael Teoranta, Gaelic Athletics Association
STRUCTURAL ENGINEER Horgan Lynch and Partners
BUS 23
ACCESS match days only

**North Dublin**

**Gilroy McMahon Architects 1995**

**Gilroy McMahon Architects 1995**

# Claris European Headquarters

Tax incentives have made Ireland a favoured location for many of the global computer companies, including Apple's software arm Claris. Brian O'Halloran has cornered the market in these 'edge-city' headquarters buildings, with their American-inspired emphasis on image, style and a corporate culture that combines work and leisure.

This is the most spectacular of the group, inspired by a brief asking for a contextual building and by an association with Californian design architects. To corporate America, 'context' means the entire sweep of Irish history and culture, not just being in keeping with the building next door, so the inspiration for this design includes prehistoric tumuli, 'violated pyramids', dry-stone walling and 'post-medieval' town squares. Materials include marble, stone, concrete, hardwood, aluminium, steel, polished plaster, blockwork, glass – and that's just the reception area.

The building form is a two-storey rectangular office and production block with a more complex pyramidal south-east corner block containing the entrance and communal facilities. The pyramid slope is brought to the ground via wedge-shaped walls and planters. The whole is loud and brash, but with an energy and dynamism much needed in the usually drab business-park setting.

ADDRESS Ballycoolin Business Park, Ballycoolin Road, Blanchardstown, Dublin 15
CLIENT Claris (Ireland) Ltd
ASSOCIATED ARCHITECT DES Architects and Engineers
STRUCTURAL ENGINEER Ove Arup and Partners
BUS 220
ACCESS reception area open during office hours

**North Dublin**

**Brian O'Halloran and Associates 1992**

**North Dublin**

**Brian O'Halloran and Associates 1992**

**Laboratory**

This Department of Agriculture laboratory is from the early phase of Regional Classicism, and contemporary with the Children's Courthouse in Smithfield (see page 66). Its inspiration comes from the Irish rural industrial and agricultural settlements of the eighteenth century, where groups of simple buildings were arranged in a formal plan. Here a pair of tall hipped roofs, reminiscent of oasthouses or brewery buildings, indicate the two main spaces, which required extract air to be discharged 14 metres above ground. The wall to the entrance front is hinged back to create a front door perpendicular to the main central axis. The spaces within, progressing from 'dirty' exterior, through changing and washing areas, to 'clean' laboratories, are symmetrically disposed on either side of a central axis defined by the trademark rooflights of the architect, John Tuomey. The functional layout has been overlaid with curious quasi-ceremonial features: a font-like hand-washbowl stands dramatically on the main axis within the wash-up area and the rear elevation has a significant-looking central flight of stairs which in fact leads only to the boiler house.

Overall, the building makes a convincing connection between tradition, modernity and location. Comparison with later work such as the National Photography Centre (page 184) shows the architect moving away from these traditional sources towards a more obscure personal language within mainstream modernism, leaving a fertile and relevant line of development, at least for the present, unfulfilled.

ADDRESS State Farm, Abbotstown Estate, Blanchardstown, Co. Dublin
ARCHITECT IN CHARGE John Tuomey
COST IR£750,000
BUS 220
ACCESS none

North Dublin

**Office of Public Works 1985**

**Office of Public Works 1985**

# North City

**Aer Lingus Ticket Sales Office**

This is, regrettably, the only surviving example of a series of stylish shop designs carried out for Ireland's national airline in Dublin, Manchester, Dusseldorf and London (although, in Dublin, bits of the Grafton Street shop have been reused in a more recent St Stephen's Green office).

The elements of the shops were designed as a kit of parts to suit varying spaces and locations. A limited palette of natural materials – limestone and granite, oak, chromium-plated steel and leather – is used to delineate activity areas: entry, reception and information, brochure display, window display, waiting and ticket sales desks. The materials, and the use of brightly coloured hand-made rugs illustrating landscapes, give an indigenous character appropriate to an institution responsible for the projection of the national image abroad. But the elegant, minimal detailing portrays a sophisticated contemporary image worlds away from the more commonly seen 'traditional' look.

Within the tightly controlled ensemble, inventive details abound – including a winged clock and the curving counter which transforms a potentially awkward freestanding column. From the striped-stone street façade to the chrome and glass counter, there is more than a whiff of the glamour and style associated with the 'golden age of flight', the 1930s.

**North City**

ADDRESS 41 O'Connell Street, Dublin 1
CLIENT Aer Lingus PLC
BUS/TRAIN City Centre
ACCESS open

**de Blacam and Meagher Architects 1990**

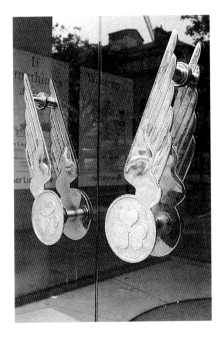

**de Blacam and Meagher Architects 1990**

# Anna Livia Sculpture and Fountain

With a series of statues and monuments distributed along its central tree-lined avenue, O'Connell Street is Dublin's only street of 'boulevard' scale and character. The latest addition is the popularly named 'Floosie in the Jacuzzi', a fountain constructed as part of Dublin's millennial celebrations in 1988 – a year-long celebration not a bit constrained by a documented history going back to AD 140.

The central bronze figure of Anna Livia – familiar from local folklore, and 'the queer old skeowsha' of James Joyce's *Finnegan's Wake* – is the personification of the River Liffey. The expressly horizontal format symbolises the journey of the river from its mountain source, through the city to the sea, and attempts to create a popular sculpture in opposition to its historic neighbours, all of which are, in the words of the artist, 'vertical, political, pompous and male'.

O'Doherty, Ireland's most prolific civic sculptor, has work displayed throughout the country. Other examples in Dublin include: the Crann An Oir (Tree of Gold) outside the Central Bank in Dame Street, Temple Bar; Gaoth Na Saile (Salt Wind) outside the Dun Laoghaire Ferry Terminal (page 260); and a kinetic wind sculpture overlooking Dublin Bay at the junction of Clontarf Road and Fairview Road, Marino.

ADDRESS O'Connell Street, Dublin 1
CLIENT Smurfit Group/Dublin City Corporation
PROJECT ARCHITECT Varming Mulcahy Reilly Associates
COST IR£200,000
BUS/TRAIN City Centre
ACCESS open

**Eamonn O'Doherty 1988**

**Eamonn O'Doherty 1988**

**Travellers' Centre**

The problem of how to give an early nineteenth-century church a new identity has been solved here by reference to the people it now serves. The change of use to a centre for travellers suggested that the new interventions should also be transitory and capable of future removal.

The interior of the church, galleried on three sides, has been left intact with the galleries boxed-in with pews to form a first floor. Into the central void has been placed a giant travellers' caravan made of corrugated iron, raised on legs and painted bright red. Access is via the second distinctive insertion, a silver tin-panelled stair tower. The new red room, in effect a building within a building, not only provides a library and workroom but also divides the surrounding space into usefully defined areas.

Original drawings show a flash gap in the floor around the perimeter of the new room to express its freestanding independence. Unfortunately the gap has not been constructed, presumably because of fire regulations, and this compromises the integrity of the original idea.

ADDRESS Free Church, Great Charles Street, Dublin 1
CLIENT Dublin Travellers' Education and Development Group
STRUCTURAL ENGINEER Pearse Associates
COST IR£300,000
BUS 22, 41A, 41B, 51A; DART Connolly
Station
ACCESS by appointment

**North City**

**McCullough and Mulvin Architects 1991**

**McCullough and Mulvin Architects 1991**

# Abbey Theatre Portico

The Abbey Theatre is Ireland's national theatre and one of the major works of the influential twentieth-century Irish architect, Michael Scott – founding father of Scott Tallon Walker. The original building was an ultra-cool Miesian box with little or no external articulation. Internally, the front-of-house facilities, concealed behind the solid façade, lacked not only daylight but a street presence. The 1991 proposal to change this – by forming a new portico to give the entrance a greater presence and to extend the lounge areas and make them visible from the street – created a stir. Battlelines were drawn between those who saw the building as a fixed work of art and those who saw change as a natural process, continually adding richness and identity to the urban experience. The architects were firmly in the latter camp. (Niall McCullough, in his recently published book *Palimpsest – Change in the Irish Building Tradition*, deals specifically with the adaption and reuse of existing buildings.)

The portico is designed to be seen as a building in its own right, co-existing with rather than extending the original building. It is also intended to relate to a pedestrianised street with a new hard-landscape layout, but this has unfortunately yet to be carried out. Despite its expressed independence, the portico nevertheless carefully follows the bay pattern of the original building and brings out the classical under-currents in the original work.

ADDRESS Lower Marlborough Street, Dublin 1
CLIENT National Theatre Society Ltd
STRUCTURAL ENGINEER Joseph McCullough and Partners
COST IR£500,000
BUS/TRAIN City Centre
ACCESS open

North City

**McCullough and Mulvin Architects 1991**

# International Financial Services Centre

In common with many European cities during the high-rolling 1980s, Dublin was perceived to need a new financial district to house the international banks and financial institutions who, it was hoped, would bring to Dublin some of the business carried out in Frankfurt or the City of London. This was coupled with an equally common need to redevelop run-down post-industrial dockland areas. The two requirements came together in a competition held in 1987 for the redevelopment of the North Wall dock area to the east of the Custom House, with the Liffey to the south and the urban badlands of Sheriff Street to the north and east. The total site, amounting to about 11 hectares of land, contained historic buildings and dock structures, and much dereliction.

The competition was won by Burke-Kennedy Doyle, one of Ireland's largest architectural firms, in association with American architects Benjamin Thompson, best known for the docks revitalisation in Boston. The first phase, fronting on to Custom House Square, was constructed with enormous speed and completed in 1990; development recommenced in 1996 and most of the remaining buildings are now either under construction or about to begin. The end result will be a collection of new and restored buildings for offices, housing, retail, hotel and leisure uses. It is the biggest commercial development in Dublin and the first instance since the Liberty Hall tower block (1964) on the other side of Custom House Square that the pressures of mainstream speculative development have impacted in a major way on the central area.

The site's frontage on to Custom House Square could not be more sensitive, facing as it does James Gandon's Custom House of 1791 and Michael Scott's Busaras of 1950, two of the most important architectural monuments in the city. The new buildings are a straightforward exercise in commercial design intended to impress a corporate client. The first

North City

**Burke-Kennedy Doyle; Benjamin Thompson and Associates 1990**

**Burke-Kennedy Doyle; Benjamin Thompson and Associates 1990**

buildings are well detailed with high-quality materials and finishes, making extensive use of green tinted glass and stone cladding with arcading at ground level. Their role and position in the Dublin townscape are less assured: the convex frontage muscles in on the existing buildings like a brash newcomer demanding attention. The chance to make a convex form in response to the sweep of the crescent and as a backdrop to the Custom House has been overlooked in favour of a symmetrical arrangement of blocks that looks forced on a site characterised by a natural asymmetry.

Within the site, the same heavy-handed approach is taken with the individual speculative office buildings – of solid but unexceptional design – disposed around it. These freestanding orthogonal blocks fronting the roads are all self-sufficient and inward-looking – with air-conditioned and hermetically sealed internal environments, often with their own central atrium or courtyard – but they do not make any particular attempt at place-making beyond symmetry with the original dock structures. We visited on the proverbial windswept rainy day and found that the external environment offers no shelter or respite, with the high buildings and open expanses of water forming an unforgiving microclimate. Perhaps final judgement should be withheld until the development is complete. The conversion of the Stack A warehouse (by Michael Collins and Associates), a building on a heroic scale, is about to start, and Jury's Hotel, also by BKD, has just been completed – both of which will bring people and leisure activities to the site. The landscaping installations are similarly unfinished, although extensive use of the 'Euro-bollard' and other ubiquitous pieces of mass-produced Victoriana currently being installed fails to match the scale and robustness of the surviving dockland relics. To the rear of the site the housing is gathered around the Inner Dock, neatly

**Burke-Kennedy Doyle; Benjamin Thompson and Associates 1990**

zone'd away into its own area where it does not complicate letting arrangements for the office buildings.

The problems of creating successful urban design for this type of development should not be underestimated – one only has to look at the disaster of London Docklands. Because this is an Enterprise Zone, planning permission did not have to be gained in the normal way, and the developer-led design team would have been under immense pressure to produce a conventional low-risk scheme familiar to multinational corporations worldwide. It should be no surprise, therefore, that the development has a placeless mid-Atlantic character at odds with the Dublin scene.

ADDRESS Custom House Quay, Dublin 1
CLIENT Custom House Docks Development Company Ltd
STRUCTURAL ENGINEER Ove Arup and Partners
COST IR£300 million, on completion
BUS near Busaras
DART Connolly Station
ACCESS general area: open; buildings: by appointment

**Burke-Kennedy Doyle; Benjamin Thompson and Associates 1990**

North City

**Burke-Kennedy Doyle; Benjamin Thompson and Associates 1990**

**Stack B Offices**

This low-key building might easily be overlooked in a cursory glance along the quay, but its pedigree is evident in the simple but sophisticated detailing. It is a straightforward speculative office block, part of the huge Custom House Dock development which surrounds it. Its distinctly schizophrenic character stems from the partial reuse of an eighteenth-century warehouse. The new front and west façades are a parapet-walled exercise in Kahnian brickwork – minus the arches – with the roof entirely suppressed. A grid of deep-set small windows with granite linings to head and sill are offset by a few larger openings with window frames set flush with the external wall. A lead-covered bay projects from a three-storey-high opening, with recessed and flush glazing above and below adding further to the play of planes. The interplay of shadows on the deep-set windows and their asymmetrical glazing bars gives life and movement to the façade. Similar games are played on the side elevation where the entrance door is underplayed within a two-storey-high opening.

To the rear it is a roof-dominated building with large glazed areas and the retained warehouse wall. The difference between the front and rear façades is startling, and the source of much comment. The front could be read as relating to the river and the city beyond, while the rear associates more with the historical dockland setting. Such a mixed contextual approach leaves what is only a small building struggling to hold itself together.

ADDRESS Custom House Quay, Dublin 1
CLIENT Mr D O'Brien
COST IR£3 million
BUS near Busaras; DART Connolly Station
ACCESS by arrangement with office users

**de Blacam and Meagher Architects 1996**

**North City**

**de Blacam and Meagher Architects 1996**

# The Black Church Conversion

The original church – 'black' refers to the colour the calp stone from which it is built turns in the rain – was designed by John Semple in 1830 and deconsecrated in 1962. Since then, abandoned in one of the toughest areas of the inner city, it has had a chequered career. At one point it was a printworks – the eponymous Black Church Print Studios now in Temple Bar (see page 156) – and at another a busy hive for traffic wardens. The current occupiers bought the listed structure in 1990 and have converted the shell to offices.

The original building is notable for many reasons, not least as a rare outbreak of expressionistic gothic in a predominantly classical city. Its chief internal glory is the dramatic and unusual parabolic stone vault, the profile of which is emphasised by the rows of lancet windows that curve with the walls. The conversion to offices has been skilfully carried out with light steel mezzanines and an open plan which does not interfere with the reading of the original space. All the new work is clearly expressed as modern inserts into the historic volume, with the large central void allowing the space and vault to be clearly read.

ADDRESS St Mary's Place, Dublin 1
CLIENT Penco Insurances and MGM Financial Services
STRUCTURAL ENGINEER Eamon Doyle Associates
COST IR£350,000
BUS 11, 13
ACCESS by appointment

North City

**Dermot P Healy and Associates 1992**

**Dermot P Healy and Associates 1992**

**Point Depot National Exhibition Centre**

The National Exhibition Centre has been created out of a goods ware-house constructed in 1878. It is split into two parts, with a huge 10,000-square-metre cast-iron structured shed to the rear and a formal front building facing the river. The latter, an 8-metre-wide strip with a brick and stone arcaded elevation, was designed to allow trains through to the rear shed. In 1988 this conversion was an act of faith in a part of the city that many considered too disconnected from the centre. The arrival of the east-link toll-bridge and the spreading influence from the east of the International Financial Services Centre (see page 46) have more than vindicated the courage of the developer, as has the success and growing reputation of the venue itself.

The front and rear sections are designed (by different architects) to operate independently of the main hall, which is entered separately from the north. This hall was originally three linear adjacent sheds. To make them into a clear-span structure, possibly the largest structural beams ever erected in Ireland – 55 metres long by 3.5 metres high – have been added to the roof. The main external limestone walls, echoing the theme of the front building, have been kept and the industrial character of the original building maintained where possible.

The strip to the south overlooking the Liffey is architecturally the more interesting building, with the new works treated as insertions into the existing spaces. Although clearly new and different, they are always compatible, with exposed steelwork and chunky detailing finding parallels with the riveted-iron original beams and robust brick and stone materials. The ground floor retains the original 8-metre-high bays where the trains used to pass through the building and out of the arched front arcade. These bays have been used to create mezzanine platforms for the two bars on either side of the central entrance lobby to the main hall. The

**Shay Cleary Architects/Stephen Tierney and Associates 1988**

North City

**North City**

**Shay Cleary Architects/Stephen Tierney and Associates 1988**

mezzanines not only connect the bars but also neatly circumvent licensing restrictions on the use of the entrance lobby.

At first-floor level a restaurant, reached by a rather obscure staircase from the central lobby, runs the full width with an enfilade of rooms serviced from a central bar. The restaurant space is infused with the wonderful Dublin light, the crystal-clear quality further enhanced by the proximity of the river. A long row of identical tall windows casts bright patches across the floor, and the hard surfaces and tall uncluttered spaces have a character reminiscent of a Vermeer painting. The choice of materials complements this quality with great sensitivity, both within the restaurant and the bars, where shiny stainless steel and sharp prismatic forms create a buzzing, metropolitan atmosphere.

ADDRESS Point Depot, North Wall, Dublin 1
CLIENT Henry Crosbie
ARCHITECT restaurants and bars, Shay Cleary Architects;
concert hall, Stephen Tierney and Associates
STRUCTURAL ENGINEER Colquhoun and Partners
BUS 53A
ACCESS bar and restaurants open; main hall open for events only

**North City**

**Shay Cleary Architects/Stephen Tierney and Associates 1988**

**North City**

**Shay Cleary Architects/Stephen Tierney and Associates 1988**

## Centre for the National League for the Blind

The area around Gardiner Street and Mountjoy Square has become the most run-down of all the central areas of Dublin. Once one of the more fashionable areas, it has been particularly damaged by the north-south partition of the city, with the south developed as affluent middle-class business districts and the north abandoned to poverty and dereliction. But slowly this is being turned around and new housing schemes are springing up amongst the ruins. The tattered remains of Gardiner Street Lower have recently been partially reinstated by a desperate pseudo-Georgian flats development, but further up the street more adventurous public housing schemes by the National Building Agency are appearing on the vacant urban blocks around the junction with Séan MacDermott Street Upper. These neat four-storey perimeter developments are enlivened by expressive brick detailing with an Amsterdam School flavour.

Behind Mountjoy Square, the new centre for the NLB stands as a brick fortress against the threat of vandalism. Within its main elevation it carries a wistful comment on the realities of building in this toughest of environments: a curiously graphic, stylised 'cutaway' through the blank brick sheath which reveals a glass curtain-walled building behind, indicating a desire for a Miesian box, tempered by the realities of site, and resulting in a metaphor for a building used predominantly by the blind.

ADDRESS Hill Street/Gardiner Place, Dublin 1
CLIENT National League for the Blind
STRUCTURAL ENGINEER John McShane
COST IR£450,000
BUS 40A, 40B, 41A, 41B, 41C; DART Connolly Station
ACCESS restricted

**North City**

**E N Smith and Kennedy Architects 1994**

**E N Smith and Kennedy Architects 1994**

**Offices**

Although only seven years old, this building is already something of a museum piece, reflecting a period in Dublin when emphasis was placed on the development of a modern classical urban style based on Georgian precedent. At the time of its construction, the quays were in a terrible state of neglect after years of blight caused by plans for road widening along the Liffey (see page 82). This building was one of the first instances of low-key contextual response to the repair of the city's shattered fabric, an approach which now has almost universal acceptance. It was also one of the first examples of what has since become the Dublin modern vernacular: the classical language of plinth, *piano nobile*, cornice and attic storey.

A gothic ground-floor granite façade remained from the site's previous occupant, a Presbyterian church, and this has been retained as the plinth of the new façade. The ruin is wrapped up in the new elements, which are designed to harmonise with the neighbouring bank building. Lurking rather perversely in the centre of the façade is a fragment of an International Style nautical white design, as if the architects were struggling to repress the urge to be modern.

More recent work by the same architects, in equally historic settings – the Parsons Building extension at Trinity, for instance (page 234) – is altogether more contemporary in approach, suggesting, perhaps, that this diversion into the past proved to be a cul-de-sac.

ADDRESS Ormond Quay, Dublin 1
STRUCTURAL ENGINEER Thomas Garland and Partners
BUS 51, 51B
ACCESS none

**North City**

**Grafton Architects 1989**

**Grafton Architects 1989**

# Irish Distillers Group Headquarters

The head office of the Irish Distillers Group, producers of Jamieson and Powers whiskey, is an important early example of conservation and urban renewal. At the time of construction it was usual for such headquarters to be sited in a greenfield or suburban location in a purpose-designed building. Irish Distillers chose instead to build next to the old Jamieson distillery in Smithfield, one of the more run-down areas of the north side of the river. The client also insisted that the new building include the conservation and conversion of two fine existing warehouses on the site, and that it should respond positively to the decayed but historic context.

This act of faith in the city has been rewarded with a design that subtly responds to the visual requirements of the brief. The main entrance, at the return of the L-shaped block, faces a newly landscaped forecourt surrounded by railings and facing Smithfield Square. The stone walls have been updated with groupings of openings edged with dressed stone, and contemporary projecting oriel windows. The entrance itself, within a fan-shaped curtain-walled insertion, displays more than a touch of Alvar Aalto in its form. The rear elevations are comfortably at home in the dramatic canyon of Bow Street and use the stone walls of the old buildings to mediate between the distillery and the ancient church of St Michan.

The now-derelict main distillery site next door is soon to be redeveloped as a large-scale mixed-use scheme by A+D Wejchert.

ADDRESS Bow Street, Dublin 7
CLIENT Irish Distillers Group
STRUCTURAL ENGINEER Rooney McLoughlin Associates
COST IR£2 million
ACCESS none

**Brian O'Halloran and Associates 1979**

**Brian O'Halloran and Associates 1979**

**Children's Courthouse**

The Children's Courthouse was the first significant building from the neo-rationalist group from UCD. John Tuomey, back in Dublin after four years with James Stirling in London, carried out this scheme while with the OPW. The design was conceived as a demonstration of contextual urban repair as well as an architectural expression of a civic institution.

The new building picks up the existing parapet heights and rebuilds the corner of the old Jamieson distillery complex. Within that overall restraint the building is articulated to reflect its own use and internal layout. The front entrance opens on to a central stair leading up to the twin courtrooms, themselves articulated as separate volumes on the side elevation. The main internal spaces are rigidly formal and processional, and the whole design is steeped in the Irish neo-classicism that had become part of the growing contextual awareness.

There has been much debate on whether this is an appropriate architectural expression for a juvenile courthouse. Many have felt that the formalism of the building symbolises a reactionary return to less humanitarian times – and the unfortunate similarities between the roof-level glazed canopy and a gallows have not gone unnoticed. The architect has possibly overstated the case in an effort to reflect the *gravitas* of the building and its role as urban 'monument'.

ADDRESS Smithfield, Dublin 1
CLIENT Office of Public Works
ARCHITECT IN CHARGE John Tuomey
STRUCTURAL ENGINEER Donald Keogan Associates
COST IR£1.4 million
ACCESS public areas open

**Office of Public Works 1987**

**Stanhope Street Refuge**

Housing associations are a small but growing part of Dublin's social housing scene. This early example provides family homes and single-person flats in a tight mix in and around an existing convent building. Constructed to a miserly budget on a site constrained at every turn, the scheme nevertheless manages to utilise a range of urban design elements to forge a coherent piece of city.

Passing through the existing convent gates you enter the arrival space of Stanhope Green, with the former convent to the right and a simple terrace of family houses to the left, canted to allow a view to the new convent (by different architects, with less interest in urban space). The new housing makes reference to the local terraced cottages, but is overlaid with an arcade rhythm that declares a rationalist inclination.

A further, more private, space is reached through the convent building, and contains the single-person flats and workshops. This courtyard is a miniature town square, with a formality that belies the small scale. Arcades run down the two long sides, column spacing is reflected in the paving grid, and its end elevation is one of studied asymmetry. Ordinary materials and elements of construction are raised above the mundane by careful consideration and the ambition to make the whole greater than the sum of the parts.

ADDRESS Stanhope Street, off Grangegorman Lower, Dublin 1
CLIENT Focus Housing Association
STRUCTURAL ENGINEER Fearon O'Neill Rooney
ACCESS to Stanhope Green; by appointment elsewhere

**Gerry Cahill Architects 1991**

North City

North City

Gerry Cahill Architects 1991

# Technical College Extension

'Bolton Street' is one of Dublin's two schools of architecture; it also provides courses in a wide range of other professional and trade disciplines. The original building, formerly a hotel, is a simple courtyard plan with a 'race-track' circulation system on various levels. The architects' brief for the extension was to provide 8000 square metres of new space for a mixed bag of lecture, seminar, studio, office and library uses. The subplot was to transform the cold and institutional feel of the old college into something more open with a sense of place and community, where encounters between different disciplines and the cross-fertilisation of ideas could fruitfully occur.

The new work involved immense practical problems – including connecting at seven different levels to the existing building, incorporating the shells of existing buildings, and the confined nature of the site. The basic moves were to create a new entrance to the whole college (off Kings Inns Street), a central landscaped courtyard, and a new internal social space wrapping around the south and east sides of the court. The new entrance and social space plug directly on to the race-track corridors of the existing building, locking the new and old together. The larger spaces – library, canteen and main lecture room – were then positioned in the largest areas behind the social space where lightwells pierce the deep plan.

The success of the scheme lies in the way the college has been transformed by the new courtyard and social space. Since funding is available only for 'educational space', these two elements (considered unproductive areas) had to be paid for out of the circulation budget. The achievement of Bolton Street is therefore not just architectural – the main spaces were in effect a 'free' bonus.

The social space faces north with a huge sloping roof which pitches up three storeys to high-level strip glazing. This casts sunlight across the

**Gilroy McMahon Architects 1986**

ceiling plane and animates a potentially sunless area. The circulation routes, on balconies around the perimeter, all pass through this space and it becomes a touchstone when moving around the building, giving orientation and direction to a complex plan. You are less aware of the courtyard: few corridors overlook it and the large roof of the main space blocks the view. This roof is a mixed blessing in many ways – although undoubtedly a powerful spatial device when viewed from ground level, it becomes increasingly intrusive from higher up. The patterning of sunlight across its surface is, however, one of the abiding images of the building.

The careful introduction of daylight is evident throughout, with the paint scheme often acting in unison. A Scandinavian technique which uses paint in gradations of intensity has been employed in many of the public and studio spaces to increase sunlight awareness.

Externally, warm bricks, a horizontal emphasis, and aluminium windows flush with the outside face, reflect Des McMahon's continuing love affair with Scandinavian modernism. The windows vary in size and style to express the functions of the internal spaces.

The building was awarded the Triennial Gold Medal for 1986–88, Ireland's highest architectural honour.

ADDRESS Bolton Street College of Technology, Bolton Street/Kings Inns Street, Dublin 1
CLIENT City of Dublin Vocational Education Committee
STRUCTURAL ENGINEER Ove Arup and Partners
COST IR£7.5 million
BUS 11, 11A, 11B, 16, 16A, 36, 36A
ACCESS open

**Gilroy McMahon Architects 1986**

**North City**

**Gilroy McMahon Architects 1986**

# National Museum of Ireland: Collin's Barracks

Built in 1701 as the Royal Barracks to the designs of Thomas Burgh (see also page 96), these are the world's oldest continually occupied barracks. For security reasons the internal spaces have always been closed to the public, and even omitted from maps, but recently the eastern section has been vacated by the military and is to become home to the National Museum of Ireland, which is moving from its current site in Merrion Square. This work forms phase 1, and the museum facilities will continue to expand as the army progressively vacates the entire site.

Lifting the security blanket has revealed one of Dublin's finest urban spaces. The complex was originally constructed as three formal squares ranged along high ground to the north of the Liffey. The central square was demolished some time ago, but the eastern Clarke Square remains wonderfully intact, with four ranks of austere granite barracks buildings surrounding a vast drill yard. This square is pierced by central low-arched entrances, signalled with pedimented projecting bays. The western half of the square has a low arcade at ground level and this section forms the first phase of the museum conversion. The corners of the square had been demolished for ventilation during an outbreak of fever at some time in the past; the southern corners have now been reinstated with new glazed walls enclosing vertical circulation points. These low-key interventions are the only obvious external signs of the new conversion, the courtyard façades integrating better than the more abstract external walls which are in the form of a translucent Japanese screen.

Entry to the museum is through the western arch, which will eventually connect to the car parks and the main approach from the original site of Royal Square. Glass doors in the arcade open into a double-height entrance lobby which introduces the language of the new conversion. The

**Gilroy McMahon Architects 1996**

**Gilroy McMahon Architects 1996**

existing buildings are a series of interconnected rooms without corridors, and this pattern has been maintained in the new work with circulation around the square side passing through a series of single- and double-height interiors which have been formed from the original spaces.

Where possible, evidence of the building's former use has been left, allowing the ancient worn surfaces to speak eloquently of their past life. The new work overlays the old and is given its own contemporary identity. By using robust, textural, self-finished materials such as polished plaster, oak, granite and even utilitarian cable-tray ceilings, a dialogue is set up between old and new, each commenting on and complementing the other. The new work has a tactile quality allied to a clarity of thought that is entirely appropriate to the character and spirit of the old buildings and which resonates in a way that a more historically correct, 'in keeping' design could not hope to achieve.

ADDRESS Benburb Street, Dublin 1
CLIENT Ministry of Art and Culture
ASSOCIATE ARCHITECTS Office of Public Works
STRUCTURAL ENGINEER Lee McCullough and Partners
COST IR£8.3 million
BUS 25, 25A, 26, 37, 39, 51, 51B, 70, 70X
ACCESS open

**Gilroy McMahon Architects 1996**

**Gilroy McMahon Architects 1996**

# Phoenix Park Visitors' Centre

The original building here, for many years home to the Papal Nuncio, was demolished in the late 1970s, leaving only the stable block and a late sixteenth-century tower house discovered during demolitions. The ground plan of the main house is now set out in hedges around the castle.

The new visitors' centre for Phoenix Park, Europe's largest urban park, has been formed from an amalgam of the existing stable buildings and new elements reinforcing the edges of the original stable courtyard. The theme of the farmyard informs the designs of all the new buildings. Entry is through the old archway from the castle side. To the left the yard has been completed by the new café. This appears to be a masonry construction but inside it is revealed to be a light timber-clad building whose curved roof is a direct reference to those ubiquitous steel-framed barns. Opposite the café on the axis of the courtyard is the main visitors' centre, entered via the glazed arch of the existing building. At the rear of this building lies the main architectural intervention, a linear block separated from the older building by a glazed arcade strip. This again contrasts lightweight construction and curved forms with the older masonry buildings. Externally the new buildings are clad in Irish Douglas fir, the end elevations of the north block in particular forming a complex sculptural mass.

ADDRESS Nunciature Road, off Chesterfield Avenue, Phoenix Park, Dublin 8
CLIENT Office of Public Works
ARCHITECTS IN CHARGE Ciaran O'Connor and Gerard O'Sullivan
STRUCTURAL ENGINEER O'Connor Sutton Cronin
COST IR£900,000
BUS 10 from city centre
ACCESS open 9.30–17.00 every day; admission charge

**Office of Public Works 1992**

**Office of Public Works 1992**

# The Quays

# The Quays

The fortunes of the quays have mirrored the fate of the city as a whole in recent times. Lining both sides of the Liffey, from Phoenix Park in the west to the Custom House in the east, the quays form the heart and soul of the city, with the finest neo-classical monuments jostling the Georgian grain in an inimitable balance of uniformity and variety. The *Architectural Review*, in its special number of November 1974 championing the issue of Dublin's neglect, stated: 'In Dublin it is not so much the famous Georgian streets and squares, fine as they are, that one remembers, but the unifying presence of the Liffey ... the house-lined waterway form[ing] a powerful yet endearing image, strong but at the same time human in scale and given a special poignancy by the limpid Dublin light.'

Extraordinary as it now seems, the whole ensemble was threatened with wholesale demolition for road-widening, and a blanket of planning blight was lowered over the entire area for three decades. As recently as 1991 first-rate Georgian houses were still – scandalously – being demolished at Arran Quay. Times change, however, and now a brighter future is promised following the wholesale reconstruction of the quays, which has been achieved in a remarkably short time. Almost all of the derelict buildings have been restored or rebuilt, mostly following the style first modelled by Grafton Architects at Ormond Quay. The use of this 'planner-friendly', modernised neo-Georgian vocabulary has now reached epidemic proportions throughout the city, but particularly here along the quays. The very ubiquity of the style, and the lack of ambition it represents, makes it an easy target; but there is a case to be made for developing just such a standard as 'city grain' – a uniform backdrop against which the monuments of the city and the better buildings are able to shine. This is the case on the quays, where a few of the recent buildings stand out in marked contrast to their neighbours.

**Various architects**

**Various architects**

On the north bank, the largest recent development is by Zoe Properties at Bachelor's Walk, where an entire city block east of the Ha'penny Footbridge has been rebuilt as flats. The fakery of the elevations on to the quays is quite convincing from a distance, but on closer inspection is let down by the hopeless 'classical' detailing and sudden changes of style on the rear and courtyard elevations. After so many years of pressing for the repopulation of the city centre it seems churlish to complain when it finally begins; but this scheme, because of its sheer density and paucity of public space, can hardly be considered a model of its type.

Further upstream, on Ormond Quay and towering above its neighbours, is the building designed by architects Shaffrey Associates to house their own offices and home. The Amsterdam-style brick building is notable for its heavy roof forms and mosaic details which take their lead from the exuberant Sunlight Chambers building of 1901 opposite.

At the corner of Ormond Quay and Arran Street is Equity House by David Crowley Architects, neatly detailed in a style halfway between the traditional and the contemporary, which makes an event of turning the corner. The northern quays are terminated at Ellis Quay by possibly the neatest exercise in 'planners' style' by Burke-Kennedy Doyle, where the usual mix of elements is held together by a sure touch and satisfactory proportions.

The south side running from west to east is dominated initially by the Guinness Brewery and a stretch of river frontage still awaiting investment. It contains an extraordinary, cartoon 'Palladian-style' petrol station with the dubious accolade of being so awful that it is noteworthy.

By the time Merchants Quay is reached things have improved. The exotic copper gates to Marshalsea Court add style to a simple building, and a residential development in three-colour-render blocks by O'Muire

**Various architects**

**Various architects**

Smyth Architects uses bays and balconies to make the most of river views. The curve in the river at Woodquay is dominated by the Civic Offices (page 208) and adjacent Viking Centre (page 204), soon to be joined by a new housing development by the museum's architects Gilroy McMahon – all part of the Temple Bar area which spills on to the river frontage at Wellington Quay. The Clarence Hotel has been newly restored as Dublin's first 'designer' hotel (in the style of the Royalton in New York) by Costello Murray Beaumont Architects, and The Cobbles development by Douglas Wallace uses the ubiquitous central columned windows with curved steel balconies to raise the game of an otherwise ordinary block of flats. The rectilinear white façade and exuberant roof forms of the Temple Bar Gallery (page 152) prove that the 'planners' style' need not be the only solution for infill sites.

The scale of the architecture gradually increases as one approaches O'Connell Bridge and the main commercial centre with its grouping of mainstream office developments among older Victorian remnants. Beyond the barrier of the railway bridge, the quays end at George's Quay, newly reconstructed by Keane Murphy Duff Architects. The most unfortunate aspect of this development is not so much the banality of the design but the fact that it destroys the balance between monument (in this instance, James Gandon's Custom House opposite) and small-scale grain which continues to characterise the rest of the quays.

**The Quays**

BUS 25, 25A, 26, 37, 39, 51, 51B, 66, 66A, 67, 67A, 70, 70X

**Various architects**

**Various architects**

# South City

# The Irish Museum of Modern Art

The Royal Hospital, Kilmainham, was the first major classical building in Ireland, constructed to designs by Sir William Robinson in 1680 – at the time of the birth of the classical city – and masterminded by the then Lord Lieutenant, the Duke of Ormonde. It was built to house retired soldiers (on the model of Les Invalides in Paris), and has a very satisfactory rational and quadrangular plan.

The north range contains the Dining Room and Chapel; on the other three sides, ranks of rooms on three storeys are separated by massive chimney stacks which form smaller closets and antechambers. Corridors around the courtyard edges give access, and the ground floor forms an external arcade with stairs at the corners. The complex is surrounded by 16 hectares of landscaped grounds facing the contemporary Phoenix Park across the Liffey to the north. The buildings and grounds were magnificently restored in 1985, winning a Europa Nostra Award for the architects Costello Murray Beaumont. When the original plans for an Arts and Cultural Centre foundered, the building was designated the new Museum of Modern Art.

Entrance to the grounds is from the east or west: the eastern approach, from Military Road, involves a rather dark and abrupt arrival, but is the most convenient from the city centre; from the west, however, a tree-lined avenue offers a more memorable experience and reveals the building in its magnificent setting. Baroque pedimented projecting bays in the middle of each façade acknowledge the point where the approach axes enter the central square. Originally this space was grassed over and planted with trees, but the first intervention by Shay Cleary was to cover the square with gravel, thus in one move not only converting its previously domestic character into one of public urban arrival, but also reinforcing the links with its Parisian ancestor.

**Shay Cleary Architects 1991**

**South City**

**Shay Cleary Architects 1991**

The main entrance to the museum is elegantly marked by strips of granite which lead the eyes, and the feet, towards the front doors. The entrance is further signalled by the glazing of the perimeter arcade and a carefully sited row of flagpoles.

The entrance foyer is the only major change to the building in this deliberately low-key conversion. The original entrance passage and surrounding rooms have been hollowed out on the ground and first floors to create a double-height space, connected by a steel staircase. The ticket office and bookshop open off this space at ground-floor level, and the first floor is arranged as an open exhibition space. This area is contained by glazed screens which fill the arcade arches and the side approaches. But the dark grey of the frames and the pattern of the glazing bars (which pick up lines within the existing elevations) make a very abrupt relationship with the original building. An interesting comparison can be drawn with an identical situation in the Collin's Barracks conversion by Gilroy McMahon just across the Liffey (see page 74). There the new arcade glazing is treated as a separate layer and placed directly behind the arcade construction; moreover, the glazing-bar design relates more to the new layer than the old building, providing a more subtle balance without compromising the modernity of the design.

By including the area of the arcade, space has been made for a new steel stair with glass treads, the most conspicuously 'designed' element in the museum. Here too a direct approach to detailing and structure gives it a robust character – more Massey Ferguson than Eva Jiricna.

The display areas of the museum occupy three sides of the courtyard and for the most part retain the original room layouts and the rhythm of the old bedrooms and closets. These have been connected with new openings to form a sequential viewing route. The small size of the rooms

**Shay Cleary Architects 1991**

**Shay Cleary Architects 1991**

allows some works of art to be displayed individually. White walls and ceilings, light grey floors, and low-key service installations both reflect the austerity of the original building and provide the necessary neutral background for the art.

To the south of the main building the Office of Public Works (project architect, Elizabeth Morgan) has converted the nineteenth-century coach-house block into artists' studios and doubled the extent of the original buildings with a pastiche block – an example of the, sadly, inevitable compromise that results when building in such proximity to 'heritage'. It is a pity, given the confidence and skill of the modern interventions within the main building, that a bolder contemporary design could not have been achieved. The studios themselves, however, are a great resource, allowing the public to meet the artists and see demonstrations of their work.

**South City**

ADDRESS Royal Hospital, Kilmainham, Dublin 8
CLIENT Office of Public Works
STRUCTURAL ENGINEER Joseph McCullough and Partners
BUS 68, 68A, 78A, 90; Nipper Bus 1, 2 and 3
ACCESS Monday to Saturday 10.00–17.30; Sunday 12.00–17.30

**Shay Cleary Architects 1991**

South City

**Shay Cleary Architects 1991**

# Dr Steevens' Hospital Restoration

Dr Steevens' Hospital was constructed in 1720 to the designs of Thomas Burgh, along similar lines to Kilmainham Hospital on the hill behind (see page 90) and the Collin's Barracks across the Liffey to the north, also by Burgh (page 74). The building, in use as a hospital until 1987, has now been converted to office use. Its principal historic features, in particular the central arcaded courtyard, have been restored, but there is much that is new – surprising, perhaps, at first glance.

The 'restored' yellow ochre north elevation is, in fact, a new addition to the Dublin townscape, as is the forecourt between the frontage and the adjacent Heuston Station. In this area the original north façade had been hidden behind the clutter of two centuries of hospital extensions. Along with the removal of these buildings, the main entrance was moved from its original position in the east façade, under the clock tower, to the centre of the north façade. The new entrance, however, is a copy of the former classical entrance – a disappointingly timid solution given the quality of the modern interventions at both neighbouring buildings and the architect's own modern pedigree. Nevertheless, the newly disclosed façade is a fine thing; moreover, due to the unusual scale and disposition of windows in the pediment, it also manages to incorporate a distinctly Irish quality in its classicism.

ADDRESS Steevens Lane, Dublin 8
CLIENT The Eastern Health Board
STRUCTURAL ENGINEER Joseph McCullough and Partners
COST IR£4.4 million
BUS 24, 68, 69, 79
ACCESS by appointment only

**Arthur Gibney and Partners 1992**

**Arthur Gibney and Partners 1992**

# Allingham Street Housing

The provision of social housing by housing associations is a developing idea in Dublin with, as yet, few built schemes. Gerry Cahill has been at the forefront of the genre since the early days, but has little in the way of built work to show for it.

Allingham Street has been completed, however, providing 14 three-storey houses and 27 flats. With their rather suburban-looking brick and pale-yellow render, the flats form 'gateposts' to the new street. The brick terrace of houses that forms the north side of the cul-de-sac is of a more satisfactory design, having a regular rhythm of identical façades with projecting ground-floor porches and generous steel balconies to the first-floor living rooms, which face the street rather than the more usual garden side. This gives the balconies a southerly aspect and allows for communication between the living rooms and the street. The scheme also includes a communal room for use by the residents, although during our visit this role was being provided by the street itself. A lively and developing interaction between the public areas and the balconies is laying the foundations for a true neighbourhood community.

ADDRESS Allingham Street, The Liberties, Dublin 8
CLIENT NabCo, The Co-operative Housing Association
STRUCTURAL ENGINEER Fearon O'Neill Rooney
COST IR£1.85 million
BUS 50, 56A, 77, 77A, 150, 210
ACCESS none

South City

**Gerry Cahill Architects 1995**

**Gerry Cahill Architects 1995**

# Solicitors' Office Extension

A tiny rear office extension, on a side alley within a tough area of the Liberties, is not normally the recipe for a stylish piece of architecture, but this one transcends normal expectations. The familiar elements of Tynan's vocabulary are all here – red brick, carefully proportioned and elegantly thin steel windows, notched planar surfaces, and corner windows. The new work extends an existing corner building and, apart from a ground-floor reception area, provides individual office spaces for the lawyers. The building form is carefully modelled to avoid the windows on the rear elevation of the main building and to open up the first-floor offices for maximum light penetration and the view back to busy Francis Street.

Internally the rear top-lit circulation route emphasises the nature of the long, narrow site. The small area available for circulation has been manipulated to form a complex double-height space and bridge link, expanding the space within.

ADDRESS 32 Francis Street, Dublin 2
CLIENT Garrett Sheehan
STRUCTURAL ENGINEER DBFL
COST IR£135,000
BUS City Centre
ACCESS none

South City

**Derek Tynan 1995**

**Derek Tynan 1995**

**Patrick Street Housing**

This is the longest street frontage constructed by a single developer in Dublin since the end of the eighteenth century. Construction of the 195 flats and seven shops was in two phases with the greater density of the second phase to the south showing in the additional attic storey and increased height. While the individual elements of the blocks refer to their Georgian forerunners, the overall scale is more akin to the Victorian tenements of the Iveagh buildings opposite. The great joy of a Georgian terrace is the interplay between the broad uniformity and unity of the whole, and the detail which expresses the differences between the houses. The new terrace adopts the traditional kit of parts – rusticated plinth with brick walls above, flat parapets and metal balcony details – which gives a certain unity but misses out the variety of detail. Although many of the accepted rules of townscape design have been followed – corners are celebrated, entrances are expressed, the top floor is set back – they fail to disguise the sameness of the flats behind. Their equal floor and window heights and unvarying repeated details undermine the intended 'Georgian' reading of the façade. This is particularly true of the second phase; the earlier Ardilaun Court has more satisfactory overall proportions.

ADDRESS Patrick Street, Dublin 7 (from Dean Street to St Nicholas Place)
CLIENT Astondale Developments Ltd
STRUCTURAL ENGINEER O'Connor Sutton Cronin
COST IR£6.5 million
BUS 50
ACCESS none

**Fitzgerald Reddy Associates 1994**

# Bride Street Housing

The influence of the adjacent Dutch-gabled Iveagh buildings of 1894 can be seen in this high-density housing scheme, constructed as part of the much wider reconstruction of the whole Christchurch area.

Fifty-nine flats and maisonettes are squeezed on to less than half a hectare, with a large-scale L-shaped corner block along the site frontage and a mews terrace behind. The street blocks, two-storey maisonettes on two levels with the entrance stairs and balconies stacked up into boldly modelled façades, are topped with large copper-clad barrel-vault gables. The corner of the L is enlivened by a mild outbreak of the baroque in the form of twisting metal stairs and glass-block walls. Terracotta plaques on the walls commemorate *Gulliver's Travels* – Jonathan Swift having once been a local resident. An archway leads through to the rear mews terrace, which is rather dwarfed by its muscular counterpart.

The larger street-front blocks herald a welcome return of scale and form in the Corporation's work, after a period in which inner-city housing schemes have been dominated by the inappropriate adoption of suburban standards and aesthetics.

ADDRESS Bride Street/Golden Lane, Dublin 8
CLIENT Dublin Corporation
ARCHITECT IN CHARGE Donal McCarthy
STRUCTURAL ENGINEER Nicholas O'Dwyer and Partners
COST IR£3.25 million
BUS/TRAIN City Centre
ACCESS none

**South City**

**Dublin Corporation City Architects 1995**

**Dublin Corporation City Architects 1995**

# Dublin Castle Restoration and Conference Centre

Dublin Castle has been continuously occupied for 1000 years (for 700 of which it formed the seat of the English administration in Ireland) and has building fabric extant from all ages of its development. After a period of recent neglect the castle became a focus for considerable restoration efforts and rebuilding. It is now open to the public, mostly as a tourist attraction, but it also includes various government facilities. Amongst the restored historical buildings and interiors are large sections of new work, notably Castle Hall (which also includes the European Hall, the new government conference centre constructed for the EEC summit in Dublin in 1990). An important new pedestrian route through to Ship Street, via the kitchen building and the new garden area at the rear, has added permeability to the building mass.

The heart of the castle is the Upper Yard, entered via a baroque gateway in Castle Street. Upon entry you become aware that the gateway is one of a matching pair on either side of Bedford Tower, the former Genealogical Office and now renamed Castle Hall. (Originally intended as the visitors' centre, this is now located in the vaults in Lower Yard.) The two gates are known as Justice and Fortitude. Until recently the latter was a dummy, with access blocked by a bank building on Castle Street. Now the route from Fortitude Gate to the street has been opened for the first time, allowing visitors to pass (via a new bridge over a low-level water garden in the position of the old moat) down to new gates into the street. From the bridge, the extension seen to the rear and right of Bedford Tower is Castle Hall; to the left at the end of the 'moat' is the European Hall.

Returning to the Upper Yard and turning right, the archway through the existing buildings leads to George's Court, a new landscaped area. This continues to the right up stairs on to a roof garden over the confer-

**Office of Public Works 1989**

ence centre, from where there is a good aerial view of the new work. Turning left out of George's Court leads to a new route out of the castle to the south, dropping down various levels to Ship Street.

This brief journey has passed through a very complicated mass of buildings. In resolving all this, the architects had to face many challenges – fitting modern facilities into an ancient setting, restoring existing buildings as well as building new ones, and making sense of any archaeological finds. Throughout this work, various historical levels have been uncovered and old walls and other fragments revealed for the first time. The architects have also been mindful of retaining the historical uses of some of the spaces; for example, they have reinterpreted the gardens which previously extended around the area of the old moat.

The new buildings manifest themselves as heavy-looking, striped, grey-granite blocks which, when required, pick up existing cornice and stringcourse lines that allow them to settle into their locations without resorting to all-out pastiche. The main new external space is around the bridge beyond Fortitude Gate, where the two main new internal volumes face each other across the water garden. Their windows, based on square modules, and vaguely post-modern details betray the design as late 1980s vintage. The gold window frames and Chinese-style bridge and balustrading do not seem at home in a castle setting; they bring to mind, instead, contemporary Arabic houses. Taken as a whole, however – with the interaction between old and new, the horizontal layering of the construction (including the reuse of the arcade from the old bank), the fountains and the sculpture – a fine new space has been fashioned.

The striped-granite motif recurs throughout the Castle precinct to indicate new construction. The building stepping down from George's Court to Ship Street was planned as modern ramparts adjacent to the thirteenth-

**Office of Public Works 1989**

century Birmingham Tower. The ability to walk continually over and under the internal spaces, thus gaining various vantage points and unusual views, provides a continuation of the castle character. Where possible the latest work makes explicit the historic layering of the place, often by using new elements to reinterpret former features; the water garden reflects the moat location, for example.

The route to Ship Street leads to the latest areas of restoration and the newly created castle gardens. The base of the stairs at Birmingham Tower faces the Clock Tower Building and, to the right, the Great Ship Street Barracks, both recently restored. During this work the fine late-Georgian façades to Great Ship Street were revealed. The Clock Tower Building, now facing a gravel forecourt, was designed by Francis Johnson, one of the most important early nineteenth-century Irish architects. Its austere façade conceals a new central glass-roofed atrium and exhibition building which houses the Chester Beatty Library collection of books and manuscripts. Entry to the building is via a side entrance from the adjacent Dubh Linn (Gaelic for 'black pool' and the origin of Dublin's name) Garden. The pool is traditionally held to have been on the site of the new gardens, between the screen wall to the street and the Gothic Revival coach house to the south. The principal feature of the gardens is a large circular lawn within a square area. This not only reinstates a lost historic feature but also doubles as a helicopter landing pad. (Landing lights are incorporated into the interlocking Celtic serpent design in the grass.) A curving brick rampart connects a ramp to the existing bridge across to the main castle buildings.

The four corners of the space are devoted to smaller themed gardens, the most formal of which creates the entrance to the exhibition building. This is a brick box, enlivened by blind arcading, separated from the Clock

**Office of Public Works 1989**

**South City**

**Office of Public Works 1989**

Tower Building by a glass link which announces the internal atrium. To the south the gothic-revival coach house has also been restored as overflow conference facilities.

Throughout the castle precinct, all the buildings and grounds are furnished with artworks and specialist fittings commissioned from some of Ireland's leading artists and craftsmen. In their totality, the castle precincts form a rich and varied series of urban spaces surpassed in Dublin only by Trinity College.

ADDRESS main entrance in Castle Street, off Dame Street, Dublin 2
CLIENT Office of Public Works
ARCHITECTS IN CHARGE Conference Centre, Klaus Unger; Great Ship Street Barracks and Clock Tower Building, Kevin Wolahan; Dubh Linn Gardens and Coach House, David Byers
BUS/TRAIN City Centre
ACCESS no access to buildings except Chester Beatty Library from June 1997. Information available from Dublin Castle Visitors' Centre, Lower Yard

**South City**

**Office of Public Works 1989**

**South City**

# Dame Street Apartments

Known colloquially as the 'Yoke on the Oak' because of their location over The Oak public house, these flats illustrate yet another type of housing experiment within the Temple Bar city-living 'laboratory'. Here the new dwellings are placed directly on top of the host building, without any messing about to 'fit in' or 'match existing materials'. While not the most subtle of approaches, in this case it is what generates the interest.

With its terne-coated steel cladding glinting in the sun and large areas of glazing to its double-height living spaces, the block promises a secret rooftop world of light and views. Eventually the front *brise-soleil* will be covered by climbing plants, further reinforcing the notion of a hidden domain high above the street's bustle. The raking angle of the sun visor and the slope of the front glazing also strike an uplifting note, directing the gaze of the building towards the stars rather than the gutter.

ADDRESS 81–82 Dame Street, Dublin 2
CLIENT Hugh O'Regan
STRUCTURAL ENGINEER DBFL
COST IR£500,000
BUS/TRAIN City Centre
ACCESS none

South City

**Murray O'Laoire Associates 1994**

South City

**Murray O'Laoire Associates 1994**

# Dublin Institute of Technology

An eye-catching curved corner on Bishop Street marks the entry to the new Dublin Institute of Technology campus, constructed on the site of the old Jacob's biscuit factory. The site occupies an entire city block between Bishop Street and Peter Street to the north, and will be fully enclosed by new construction when the scheme is complete.

The present buildings (phase 1) include parts of the original nineteenth-century warehouses, including the ground-floor granite arcade to Peters Row which dictates the bay rhythm of the new work above. The site's previous use generated the institute's warehouse aesthetic: no-nonsense exercises in brickwork on the main elevations, and aluminium panels and windows which come alive at the corners, where drums and stepped walls resolve the geometry.

Particularly notable is the main entrance, with stepping curved screens and a patent glazed walkway at roof level making a light junction with the sky. The entrance doors open on to a triple-height entrance lobby, where a tall, raking glass screen overlooks the central campus courtyard.

**South City**

ADDRESS Aungier Street, Dublin 2
CLIENT Dublin Institute of Technology
STRUCTURAL ENGINEER Lee McCullough and Partners
BUS 14, 14A, 47
ACCESS open

**Burke-Kennedy Doyle and Partners 1994**

**Burke-Kennedy Doyle and Partners 1994**

# The Mean Fiddler Café and Music Club

The well-known Mean Fiddler café/bar is a reconstruction of the old Wexford Street Inn, a venue for traditional and folk/rock music, and the first Irish outpost of the London-based music promoter and entrepreneur, Vince Power. In a comprehensive rebuild, the shell of the old building has been partially retained to provide a ground-floor bar with an upstairs music club to accommodate 500 people. The roof has been raised and the whole structure swaddled in a hefty acoustic duvet to prevent the neighbours enjoying the entertainment.

Madigan and Donald are well known in the UK for a series of stylish modern bars and clubs, and here they use that experience to conjure up a contemporary interior from limited means. The existing street façade has been reworked with a new etched-glass screen at street level, revealing a top-lit stair leading to the main auditorium. To the rear is the ground-floor café/bar – one large room with a linear metal counter and aluminium café furniture. The use of strong colours, fair-faced materials and industrial fittings sets the character of the space and provides a rough spareness well suited to a rock venue. The wall panelling, for instance, made from directly applied plywood sheeting which is scattered with cut-out slots and coloured lighting, illustrates that a limited budget is often a stimulus for imagination and ingenuity.

ADDRESS 26 Wexford Street, Dublin 2
CLIENT The Mean Fiddler Organisation/Kieran Cavanagh Productions
STRUCTURAL ENGINEER Muir Associates
BUS 14, 14A, 47
ACCESS open

**South City**

**Madigan and Donald Architects 1995**

**South City**

**Madigan and Donald Architects 1995**

# St Stephen's Green Shopping Centre

Included here if only to answer the visitor's inevitable 'what the hell is that?' when confronted by this confection in such a prime location. It is, in fact, Dublin's 'flagship' shopping centre. Sited at the heart of the main southside shopping area, it contains three levels of shopping around a huge glass-roofed hall. To the rear lies a 650-space multi-storey car park and, below, a cavernous underground servicing area.

The main shopping hall is potentially a splendid space, but is currently choked by kitsch commercial clutter. It is also a most blatant example of the cynical developer maxim that if you trap the consumer inside with the goods (by obscuring the exits), sales increase. You can of course avoid these traps by not going in, but outside there is no escaping from the building: it muscles into every view around St Stephen's Green. The bolted-on paper-doily cladding facing the square is apparently based on a Mississippi river boat, with the vast sides and rear looking like the adjacent Gaiety Theatre on steroids.

It is shocking to realise that such a hugely important building in the life and environment of the city can have been conceived at such a banal level. However, bolt-on cladding does imply that it will also bolt off – recladding is the only hope.

If by cruel chance you find yourself trapped inside, the Diffney Menswear shop (Paul Keogh, 1989) is worth a look.

ADDRESS corner of St Stephen's Green West and Grafton Street, Dublin 2
CLIENT The British Land Company plc
STRUCTURAL ENGINEER Ove Arup and Partners
BUS/TRAIN City Centre
ACCESS open

**Power Architectural Design 1988**

**Power Architectural Design 1988**

# Millennium Countdown

This is the ambitious winner of a competition for a countdown monument to the year 2000. Centred around O'Connell Bridge, the most important link between the north and south city, it consists of a digital clock counting off the seconds to the Big Moment tethered just below the waters of the Liffey. Surrounding it are mechanical 'reeds' which are intended to emit an orchestrated sound and light display. On the bridge a steel bollard dispenses postcards printed with the time remaining to the year 2000 at the moment of purchase. At the height of the global party when the countdown reaches 000000000 this overgrown alarm clock explodes into a pyrotechnic display, becomes released from its tethers and floats out to sea ablaze as an allegory of Viking tradition (see page 142). The reeds meanwhile will have also suffered spontaneous combustion but will remain as a permanent kinetic sculpture.

The architects list their concepts as 'a study in time, the immateriality of Time and the forces of Nature, the river Liffey as the historical generator of the city and Dublin as a port ... the most beautiful and astonishing clock in the world'. After such a build-up, reality can only disappoint.

**South City**

LOCATION O'Connell Bridge
CLIENT Dublin City Corporation
BUS/TRAIN City Centre
ACCESS open

**Hassett Ducatez Architects 1996**

**Hassett Ducatez Architects 1996**

# Restaurant Tosca

Dublin is distinctly lacking in interesting new pub and restaurant interiors (though see page 202), and in this respect lags behind other European capitals. Ross Cahill-O'Brien has been behind many of the more notable recent interiors, including this eclectic exercise. He is not noted for the purity of his vision; instead he achieves effect from a concentration of ideas and images which gain in vitality what they lose in consistency.

Here the references and metaphors are well mixed: a curving art-nouveau-inspired shopfront and lobby giving way to an interior which mixes Charles Rennie Mackintosh ceilings and wainscoting with Japanese elements and modern seating. The dominant element, however, is a curious bar shaped like the bows of a ship, complete with riveted hull (made from papier-mâché and boot polish) and a magnificent figurehead cappuccino machine complete with golden eagle lurking in a tailor-made eyrie. To the nautical theme can be added the authentic touch of sea sickness if the gentle undulations of the exotic suspended lighting installation by designer Geoff Rule are watched too closely. The toilets are worth a visit too for their carefully crafted glass basins and fittings.

**South City**

ADDRESS 20 Suffolk Street, Dublin 2
PROJECT ARCHITECT Ross Cahill-O'Brien
COST IR£160,000
BUS/TRAIN City Centre
ACCESS open

**Edmondson Architects 1992**

**South City**

**Edmondson Architects 1992**

# Foyer, Department of Agriculture, Food and Forestry

The double-height foyer of a nondescript office building has been transformed with a new mezzanine structure containing meeting and conference rooms. Viewed from the street through the external arcade, its splash of yellow and bright lighting invite exploration. A freeform box raised on piloti – from the International Style stable, born of Richard Meier out of Le Corbusier – contains a conference room and is the principal focus of the space. Another is the steel and stone staircase construction which rises around a solid core at the far end, canted at an angle to the main space to emphasise the independence of the new work from the host building.

The new glass entrance canopy has a mat of Portland stone cut into the existing finishes, a touch of materiality that is not carried through into the main interior constructions, where form rather than expression of structure or material takes precedence. Serpentine seating with elegant lighting and signage completes a stylish and colourful interior in an otherwise grey Civil Service building.

ADDRESS Kildare Street, Dublin 2
CLIENT Department of Agriculture, Food and Forestry/Office of Public Works
STRUCTURAL ENGINEER Malachy Walsh and Partners
COST IR£300,000
BUS/TRAIN City Centre
ACCESS during office hours

**Shay Cleary Architects 1994**

South City

**Shay Cleary Architects 1994**

# Northern Irish Tourist Board

Strong contemporary shop interiors are a rare thing in Dublin: the norm, particularly on Nassau Street, is the heritage-style thought to be favoured by tourists. Elsewhere the contemporary approach commonly follows the minimalist model, where the architecture is invariably swamped by the merchandise.

The NITB conceals its modern heart behind a 'contextual' shopfront that is made slightly more unusual by its corner return, exploited with a new display case. Inside, by contrast, is a well-thought-out interior which draws the potential holiday-maker deep into the long thin plan. The front area, with a small arcade of brochure racks and an information desk, is aimed at the browser and information-seeker. Beyond is the main sales desk and at the end, raised up slightly, is a seating area for consultations and meetings.

A linear barrel vault in the ceiling leads the visitor in from the street and a rooflight at the back of the space pools daylight on to the meeting area. Elsewhere, illuminated walls, cherry-veneered furniture, leather seating and hand-made rugs, all within a carefully controlled colour palette, emphasise the first principle of retail design – get the customer in.

ADDRESS 16 Nassau Street, Dublin 2
CLIENT Northern Irish Tourist Board
COST IR£100,000
BUS/TRAIN City Centre
ACCESS shop hours

**South City**

**Kearney and Kiernan Architects/Michael Collins and Associates 1990**

**Kearney and Kiernan Architects/Michael Collins and Associates**

**Mercy International Centre**

This building was originally a home for distressed women, set up in 1827 by Catherine McAuley. It eventually grew into the Sisters of Mercy International, a worldwide religious organisation with the largest congregation ever established by an English-speaking founder (now buried in the garden to the rear of the buildings).

The whole complex has been restored and refurbished, a century and a half of unplanned agglomeration stripped away, and the original buildings consolidated. A new visitors' centre has been created and the chapel restored and updated. But what makes an otherwise solid and workmanlike project special is the quirky, garden elevation, designed as a scrum of little towers, each with its own character. A new brick extension with corner windows and a jaunty angled rooflight jostles an older cupola-capped bay that holds apart two towers, making them look as if they are being arrested at gunpoint. The grouping brings to mind the New York, New York Hotel in Las Vegas, where the architects have recreated a section of Manhattan without the streets. Not too many convents in Ireland provoke such outlandish associations.

ADDRESS 64A Baggot Street, Dublin 2
CLIENT Sisters of Mercy International
STRUCTURAL ENGINEER Michael Punch and Partners
COST IR£2 million
BUS 10, 46, 46A, 46B
ACCESS weekdays 11.00–16.00

**Richard Hurley and Associates 1994**

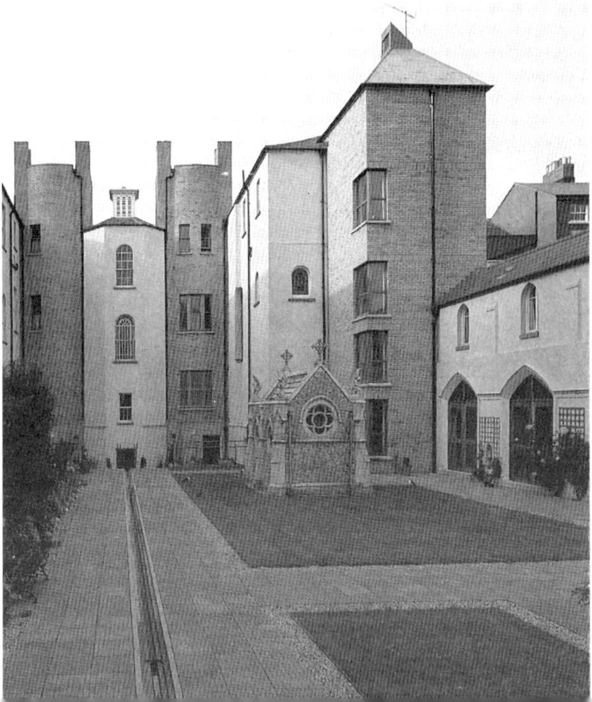

# Aranás B Offices

By and large Dublin had escaped the 1980s boom in post-modern offices – until the arrival of this building in Lower Mount Street. The site had been empty for years and sat, intriguingly, between the last of the genuine Georgian terraces running up from Merrion Square and the banal 1970s office blocks in the rest of the street.

Caught, as it were, between a rock and a hard place, the architects have avoided committing themselves to any particular architectural stand by including a bit of everything. The basic pseudo-Georgian 'contextual' façade forms a symmetrical backdrop; overlaid on to this are a vulgar 'baroque' doorway in a rusticated stone base and, at the roof, a surprisingly elegant 'modern' steel and glass oriel window.

This unholy alliance of styles is not without its successes, however, especially when viewed from a distance, when the bay window enlivens what is in reality a dull and lifeless street.

ADDRESS 65/66 Lower Mount Street, Dublin 2
CLIENT Aranás Ireland Ltd
STRUCTURAL ENGINEER Ove Arup and Partners
COST IR£2.1 million
BUS/TRAIN City Centre
ACCESS none

South City

**A+D Wejchert 1991**

**A+D Wejchert 1991**

# Waterways Visitors' Centre

This modernist object building sits in the middle of the Grand Canal Basin – a white crystalline form separate and aloof from the crumbling surroundings, with its full complement of nautical references resolutely on display. The architects had originally intended it to be a floating pontoon – until visions of the Titanic came to mind – so it has instead been constructed on concrete piles off the dock floor. Initially, the materials – white cladding and glass blocks – recall the work of American architect Richard Meier, but here the complexities of Meier's geometric response to context are bypassed in favour of a simpler game of 'pure' volumes, earning the centre the sobriquet 'the Box on the Docks'. Its sharp geometric precision is emphasised further by the warehouses, silos and other remnants of the industrial past which surround it.

The simplicity of the form is created by placing the service elements (toilets, stores, etc.) in a separate pavilion, leaving the principal building unencumbered. The service building also forms the main entrance, which leads to a bridge connecting the centre to dry land.

The main building is a simple cube, with a mezzanine on the diagonal of the square and a roof-level viewing platform. Connecting these levels is a stair housed within a glass-brick cylinder, its geometric composition creating a play between square, circle and triangle. The entrance off the bridge link is formed by cutting away the corner of the cube to reveal the glass drum. Circulation through the exhibition areas forms a carefully orchestrated architectural promenade through the internal spaces up to the roof terrace and back to the entrance via an external stair.

Internally, the walls are lined with rare quarter-sawn Irish-oak panels, and the floor with hardwood ship's decking. This soft, yacht-like interior is in sharp contrast to the building's hard exterior. Great thought was given to the admittance of daylight: the floor-level windows in particular

**Office of Public Works 1993**

**Office of Public Works 1993**

infuse the interior with reflected light. On a sunny day an energising combination of light and volume perfectly captures the intended spirit of the Modern Movement.

For some time the centre has been a beacon in a wasteland, but the whole Grand Canal area is now a focus for urban regeneration, buoyed by the success of Custom House Dock across the Liffey. The next few years should see the beginnings of a transport infrastructure, in the shape of a DART station, and new mixed-use developments with marinas, cultural institutions and watersports centres masterminded by Murray O'Laoire Associates.

ADDRESS Grand Canal Basin, Ringsend, Dublin 2
CLIENT Office of Public Works
ARCHITECT IN CHARGE Ciaran O'Connor
STRUCTURAL ENGINEER Thomas Garland and Partners
COST IR£812,300
BUS 1, 3; DART Pearse Station
ACCESS admission charged. Open June to September, 9.30–18.30 daily

South City

**Office of Public Works 1993**

**South City**

**Office of Public Works 1993**

# Clanwilliam Square Mixed Development

This small development represents a brief moment when interest in modernism was deflected by a growing interest in urban issues and historical precedent. In the late 1980s, at the end of a crippling recession, Dublin was oversupplied with office space and commercial developments were struggling to get off the ground. Allied to this was a growing recognition of the limitations of mainstream modernism, particularly in urban design. In 1988, Arthur Gibney (one-time partner of Sam Stephenson and jointly responsible for some of the most daring and controversial modern buildings in Dublin) declared the Modern Movement dead and produced Clanwilliam as the way forward.

It is a small-scale mixed development of 'own door' office units and houses arranged as streets and squares. Traditional townscape details – octagon 'gateposts' to the street entry and an emphasis on pedestrian spaces – make for a humane and appropriate model of urban development, regardless of architectural style.

The Modern Movement was not dead, however, only resting, and the best of the subsequent 'new modern' buildings (in Temple Bar, for instance) seem to have absorbed the urban lessons of Clanwilliam and put them to good effect. But when looking elsewhere (around the Custom House) it seems that Clanwilliam was merely a brief break in the clouds.

ADDRESS Clanwilliam Square, Grand Canal Quay, Dublin 2
CLIENT Slavenburg Investments Ltd
STRUCTURAL ENGINEER Joseph McCullough and Partners
COST IR£1.8 million
BUS 1, 3; DART Pearse Station
ACCESS public precinct only

**Arthur Gibney and Partners 1988**

**Arthur Gibney and Partners 1988**

# Temple Bar

# Temple Bar

The area known as Temple Bar lies at the very heart of Dublin, stretching along the south bank of the Liffey and connecting many of the country's national institutions, from Trinity College in the west to the Civic Offices and Christchurch Cathedral in the east. The medieval street pattern has survived, despite the Georgian 'Wide Streets Commissioners', and archaeological work in recent years has revealed the location of the first Dublin, built by the Vikings at Woodquay.

None of this mattered in the early 1970s, however, when – true to the spirit of the times – a large section of the area was earmarked for a massive transport interchange, part of the proposed plan (by American megapractice Skidmore Owings & Merrill) for an underground rail link to connect bus stations on both sides of the river. With a view to the grand plan, Córas Iompair Éireann (CIE), the national bus company, began buying up property in the area and leasing it out on low-cost, short-term lets. This proved a double-edged sword: many old buildings were needlessly demolished to make way for car parks and other short-term uses; but the area spontaneously developed as an unofficial bohemian centre, attracting shops, cafés, recording studios, nightclubs and art galleries. Political enthusiasm for the expensive transport interchange waned as public enthusiasm for the street culture and vibrancy of Dublin's 'Left Bank' mounted and its potential as a tourist honey-pot became more evident.

In the run-up to the 1987 elections, soon-to-be Taoiseach Charles Haughey, never a man to miss a populist move, announced he 'would not let CIE near it', and pledged his support for conservation-based development. Following his election, Haughey used Dublin's status as the 1991 Cultural Capital of Europe to secure European funds to conserve and develop the area as a cultural centre. An act of parliament established a development company – Temple Bar Properties – with a mission to stim-

ulate and facilitate the regeneration of the area by conserving the building stock and persuading the resident population to stay. In addition, the encouragement of cultural activities was given a high priority. (A limited architectural competition held in 1991 to provide a development framework for the area was concerned as much with new uses as with design.)

The recent history of Temple Bar is a reflection of the change in attitude towards the city and its conservation which has developed across Europe during the last 25 years. In Ireland, much of the architectural debate on this subject was generated by a group of architects associated with the School of Architecture at University College Dublin (UCD). The core of this debate involved both the appropriate nature of urban interventions and developments within the city, and the development of a regional architecture with a recognisably 'Irish' character. Influential in the urban debate was the work of Aldo Rossi and Leon Krier; and authors such as Niall McCullough shaped the regional debate. Although key projects – 'Dublin City Quays' of 1986 and 'Making a Modern Street' of 1991 – remained on paper, their architects (christened Group 91 at the time of the second project) went on to develop a mature and collective approach, eventually emerging as convincing winners of the Temple Bar Urban Framework competition.

Group 91's plan was based around a new east–west pedestrian route through the city blocks, enlivened by public open spaces on the gap sites previously cleared for parking. The principal spaces involved were Temple Bar Square, Meeting House Square and the new Curved Street. Use patterns, particularly the reintroduction of residential units into the inner city, were as much a part of the overall plan as formal design issues.

Temple Bar Properties were successful in encouraging the private sector, and in a relatively short period of time the area has been trans-

formed by many small-scale developments, all shaped by the overall development plan. The streetscape, too, was carefully considered, and the street furniture and art installations contribute to the unity and character of the area.

The process of development has not been without problems. Due to the sheer density of the existing building stock and complex ownership patterns, some projects became a nightmare of party-wall disputes and conflicting interests. Particular disquiet has been expressed about the wisdom of creating so many new cultural centres that will need government funding once their capital grants have been spent. The inevitable resistance to contemporary architecture within an historic area has also been expressed. As a model for urban renewal within an existing cohesive city core, the Temple Bar experiment was undoubtedly hugely ambitious, but its main objective was to improve the area without damaging the fragile spirit of place that had grown up there (largely through a lack of control or planning). Existing residents and businesses are encouraged to remain and commitments are being made to keep rents affordable. Arts and crafts and shops contributing to the streetlife are actively encouraged – but is it feasible to maintain artificially an element of anarchy? Already the ubiquitous uniformed security guards are appearing and the market forces are gathering. The area may simply be too close to the city centre to avoid the influx of building societies and corporate offices that will push prices beyond the reach of wacky shops and bazaars. How long before the buskers are auditioned by the council?

TEMPLE BAR VISITORS' CENTRE 18 Eustace Street, Dublin 2
ACCESS open 9.00–18.00 every day May to September; closed at weekends for the rest of the year

**Temple Bar Square**

Temple Bar Square is the pivotal public space on the new east–west route through the urban blocks of the area. It also sits at the important junction where the route crosses the passage between Merchant's Arch and the Ha'penny Footbridge, which links Temple Bar to the north bank of the Liffey. South of the arch, Crown Alley leads to the public space in front of the Central Bank on Dame Street.

The square contains an intricate mix of commercial and residential uses, with the building form used to articulate the exterior space. The building is, in fact, smaller than it first appears, since half the frontage to the square is a narrow strip of accommodation used principally to obscure the side of a warehouse and to form a civic front.

The side on to Fownes Street contains shops at street level with nine small flats above – performing a balancing act between the competing demands of view and light versus privacy. This generates an internal complexity which can be gauged by looking up past the large windows to the Group 91 trademark saw-tooth rooflights. Entry to the flats is through the open slot at the centre of the façade.

The elevation on to the square has six shops and a café opening on to the pavement. When closed, these premises are protected by an inventive, vertically-folding security screen, which at other times becomes a canopy. The elevation itself is a complex pattern of solid and void, with brick, glass and metal panels, and grilles within a delicate framework of steel sections. All the returns and corners are lined with aluminium or steel cover plates, depriving the brick veneer of any depth or solidity. This gives the building a fragile look, particularly when compared with the tough no-nonsense warehouses surrounding it. Describing the elevation as a stretched canvas or 'taut skin', the architects draw an interesting parallel with Georgian façades.

**Group 91 (Grafton Architects) 1995**

**Group 91 (Grafton Architects) 1995**

The external area is achieved in a simple manner by projecting a level stone surface out from the building, with tapering steps to resolve the sloping junction with Temple Bar. A few simple benches and litter bins in formal order populate the platform, and a row of tall tubular light fittings defines one edge.

The building in the square acts as an introduction to the architectural vocabulary of the new Temple Bar: mixed uses, the importance of a residential element, complex sections with monitor rooflights, open access voids connecting small entrance courts, and roof gardens – all allied to crisp modern detailing. In this case the mix gives the impression of the building as stage scenery, with the square as the stage – an effect heightened by the apparent 'thinness' of the façade skin – which is an appropriate reflection of the street-theatre ideals of the development plan.

ADDRESS Temple Bar, Fownes Street and Crown Alley, Dublin 2
CLIENT Temple Bar Properties
STRUCTURAL ENGINEER Roughan and O'Donovan Engineers
COST IR£1.1 million
BUS/TRAIN City Centre
ACCESS open

**Temple Bar**

**Group 91 (Grafton Architects) 1995**

**Group 91 (Grafton Architects) 1995**

# Temple Bar Gallery and Studios

For over ten years a group of artists' studios had existed on this site, one of the creative centres that had grown up in the area during the years of planning blight. In accordance with the stated aims of the Temple Bar reconstruction, the existing studios and gallery have been rebuilt and reoccupied by their previous tenants, providing a new improved facility and continuity of use. This sensitivity is also reflected in the buildings, which repair a large run-down city block by keeping what is useful and only rebuilding when necessary. The result is a hybrid mass of construction with frontages on to three streets, among which it is hard to tell where the old ends and the new begins.

Inside, 30 artists' studios (operating on a not-for-profit basis) are gathered around a top-lit central hall and stairway entered from Lower Fownes Street. Also on the ground floor is the Temple Bar Gallery. The corner on to Temple Bar Square rises to four storeys to match the scale of the open space, dropping down to three storeys on the narrow Temple Bar side. A projecting, concrete window sill acts as a cornice to emphasise the corner site. The material palette of white render and steel windows and doors echoes the industrial aesthetic of the original building (a shirt factory) and the surroundings. The roofline is broken into what the architects term 'a new landscape of prismatic forms derived from cubist painting of the early modern period'. The elevations display a similar striving for artistic content, with Mondrianesque coloured panels and other arbitrary elements tossed in at rakish angles. One is left with a sense of the triumph of style over content, with the designers' architectural preoccupations taking precedence over more prosaic matters such as solar gain, privacy and weathering.

A robust and *ad hoc* quality in the interiors suggests they will stimulate creative interaction between the artists and their workspaces. The gener-

**McCullough and Mulvin Architects 1994**

ously sized central staircase provides washroom areas and space for meetings and chance encounters between the building's occupants. An oval shaft piercing this central space allows large canvases to be hoisted up and down and permits daylight penetration and visual connection between the floors. The top floor of the stair has doors on to the roof terraces and is covered by a glass butterfly roof.

ADDRESS 5–9 Temple Bar, Dublin 2
CLIENT Temple Bar Properties
STRUCTURAL ENGINEER Kavanagh Mansfield
COST IR£1.1 million
BUS/TRAIN City Centre
ACCESS Monday to Saturday 10.00–18.00; Sunday 14.00–18.00

**McCullough and Mulvin Architects 1994**

**Temple Bar**

# Black Church Print Studios and Original Print Gallery

The Black Church Print Studios and the next-door Temple Bar Studios, also by McCullough and Mulvin (see page 152), were constructed in parallel, but the Print Studios – three floors of print-making workshops, with the double-height ground-floor Original Print Gallery forming a centre for information and education – comprise an altogether more substantial piece of work. The narrow street elevation is a gem, with a solid panel of stone (indicating a bank of small subsidiary rooms inside) played off against the floor-to-ceiling glazing of the studios themselves. Indented patterning to the stonework and the gridding of the windows allude to the printer's frame of typefaces. The top floor, set back to create a small terrace, allows adjacent parapet lines to be matched. On the ground floor, the gallery conceals its double-height space behind a heavy concrete grillage, pierced by an artfully placed blue column.

Modern architecture in Ireland is traditionally a Miesian stronghold, but these studios are an outbreak of pure Le Corbusier. Externally they reflect his early houses of the 1930s, but internally they have moved on to the 'béton brut' of La Tourette. On the rear elevation, best seen from the stair of the adjacent Temple Bar Studios, the curving staircase tower throws in a tiny slice of Ronchamp for good measure.

ADDRESS 4 Temple Bar, Dublin 2
CLIENT Temple Bar Properties
STRUCTURAL ENGINEER Kavanagh Mansfield
COST IR£330,000
BUS/TRAIN City Centre
ACCESS gallery open shop hours; studios by appointment

**Temple Bar**

**McCullough and Mulvin Architects 1994**

Temple Bar

**McCullough and Mulvin Architects 1994**

# The Green Building

Looking west from the square outside the Central Bank, the roofscape is enlivened by the sudden appearance of a range of propellers and solar panels which rise above the more conventional chimneys and mansards. These emblems of self-sufficiency mark the location of the Green Building, an ambitious attempt to create a state-of-the-art energy-efficient building on a dense urban site just 11 metres wide and 26 metres deep. Packed on to this plot is a mix of shops, offices and housing, gathered around a tapering central courtyard. This dense mix has been achieved with an imposed agenda of maximum 'greenness', covering natural ventilation; sustainable, alternative and efficient energy sources; recycled materials; and minimal $CO_2$ emissions. To tackle all these issues on an open site would be difficult enough, but to have done so in the dense, medieval heart of Temple Bar – and to a straightforward commercial brief – was ambitious indeed.

The shop units occupy the lower-ground and ground floors, with an office floor over. Above these are three storeys of flats (eight in total). A fan-shaped central courtyard with a freestanding lift is the key to the layout, providing daylight and ventilation to the deep plan. (The stack effect causes air entering at low level to rise to the glass roof for summer ventilation. In winter, cold air is admitted at roof level into a canvas pipe suspended in the courtyard, from where it drops to basement level for minimal fresh-air input.)

The building is heated by a combination of solar panels and a system which recycles ground water through a heat pump. Roof-mounted photovoltaic panels and wind generators contribute to the electrical load, and rainwater is recycled, as is all refuse. Plants and a fountain are positioned so as to reoxygenate the air, and the more conventional energy-saving strategies of heavy insulation and massive structure are also utilised.

**Murray O'Laoire Associates 1994**

**Temple Bar**

**Murray O'Laoire Associates 1994**

Computer modelling indicates that the building should use 80 per cent less energy than an equivalent standard-design building.

Inevitably the constraints of the site cause a few problems. One wonders about the effectiveness of ventilation to the bedrooms overlooking the lightwell, and the impact of the nearby lift. Summer ventilation which draws in air from street level must presumably also draw in exhaust fumes. Since this air passes through a shop unit which is open to the courtyard, it is hoped that the tenant will not be an aromatherapist or record dealer.

Architecturally, the usual desire of 'green' architects to adopt expressionist forms has been resisted, and the main street elevations are well-judged contextual infills, expressive of their internal use and enlivened by bay windows. The entire building is given distinction, however, by the use of artworks on the theme of recycling. The entrance screens are by Remco de Fau and Maud Cotter, and James Garner made the copper column casings out of reused water cylinders. His balustrading to the balconies uses old bicycle frames, giving an added dimension to the word 'recycling'. Internally, light fitting are made from television tubes and kitchens are fitted out with recycled pine and terracotta tiles.

ADDRESS Crow Street and Temple Lane South, Temple Bar, Dublin 2
CLIENT Temple Bar Properties
STRUCTURAL ENGINEER DBFL
COST IR£1.5 million
BUS/TRAIN City Centre
ACCESS to ground-floor shop units only

**Temple Bar**

**Murray O'Laoire Associates 1994**

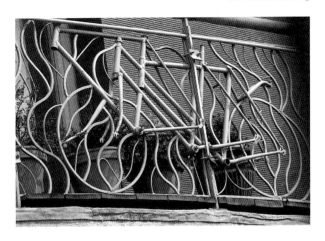

**Murray O'Laoire Associates 1994**

# Spranger's Yard Mixed Development

Spranger's Yard, on a prominent site next to the Central Bank, is another residential and retail infill development by Temple Bar Properties. It represents, however, a very different approach to the issues discussed by Group 91. Essentially an exercise in the 'picturesque', it comprises a standard over-the-shop layout with 13 shops at ground floor and 27 two-bedroom flats of similar plan on three floors. The flats line a narrow rear courtyard. The elevations are based on a traditional Irish streetscape, with colours, window types and positions, and eaves lines varied arbitrarily. Corners are turned with chamfers and balconies and the whole ensemble creates a facsimile of how the street might have looked a century ago (if you took away the modern metal sculpture which provides a spiky hair-do on the front). The building reflects the scale and grain of the area very successfully – and already looks as if it has always been there.

When comparing this scheme with, say, The Printworks (page 164) or The Green Building (page 158), the main difference is one of relative ambitions. Unlike BKD, the architects of those developments are struggling to develop building types which respond to the full range of urban issues – privacy, sunlight and daylight penetration, enclosure and view, and the hierarchy of public and private space. If the inner city is to be successfully repopulated, the same importance must be given to these issues as to the aesthetic considerations of façade and form shown here.

ADDRESS Fownes Street, Crow Street, Temple Bar, Dublin 2
CLIENT Temple Bar Properties
STRUCTURAL ENGINEER DBFL
COST IR£2 million
BUS/TRAIN City Centre
ACCESS none

**Burke-Kennedy Doyle and Partners 1995**

**Temple Bar**

**Burke-Kennedy Doyle and Partners 1995**

**The Printworks Mixed Development**

The urbane elevation on to Essex Street East conceals another complex exercise in city restoration and repair. The red-brick frontage follows the cue of its Georgian neighbours, but is subtly updated with steel windows and balustrades, and a granite-clad shopfront at street level. The focus is a two-storey entrance slot, signalled by a first-floor corner window. Here a pedestrian gate leads to a steep flight of steps whose height mysteriously conceals their destination – a raised entrance courtyard of Mediterranean character, surrounded by ten small apartments of varied type.

Of all the Group 91 residential schemes in Temple Bar, the Printworks most represents their desire to prove that 'living over the shop' is a viable and attractive form of housing for the inner city. For most of this century the centre of Dublin has been steadily depopulated as its residents moved to the suburbs – the middle class to the south and the working class to new high-rise developments to the north. The inevitable consequence of this has been a deterioration of the building stock, especially the Georgian fabric of which Dublin is made. This decay has been aided and abetted by the insistence of government authorities, particularly the fire department, that dwellings over ground-floor shops constituted a fire hazard. The problem was exacerbated by shop owners who, reluctant to take on the complications of tenants, preferred to leave the upper floors of their premises empty. Dublin is littered with examples of Georgian buildings which have been demolished from the first floor up – a sad reminder of this short-sighted attitude. By the late 1980s, the progressive architects of Group 91 saw the reversal of this trend as a major priority. In their desire to rescue Dublin from the city fathers' obsession with suburbia, considerable thought and invention were applied to alternative forms and models. The Temple Bar developments were their first opportunity to put these theories into practice.

**Group 91 (Derek Tynan Architects) 1994**

Temple Bar

**Temple Bar**

**Group 91 (Derek Tynan Architects) 1994**

The principal urban type developed was the courtyard. Raised above a ground-floor plinth of commercial space related to the street and accessed via stairs, it was part of an architectural promenade that passed from the public street to the private apartments, via the semi-public entrance court. Roof gardens and balconies attached to the dwellings provided amenity space up amongst the roofs, where sunlight and views could be exploited. This romantic notion of a secret world of light and repose high above the bustle and commotion of the street is a compelling vision, though made difficult in practice by the more mundane issues of overshadowing and lack of privacy.

The courtyard model was the one chosen for the Printworks. The architects also saw the scheme as a 'paradigm of the city' – an illustration of the cycle of construction, adaption and renewal in microcosm. This approach is revealed in the street elevation to Temple Lane, where the layering of the development can be clearly seen. Here a retained existing façade forms a two-storey commercial plinth with a terrace of three duplex flats over. However, it seems that the retention of this façade was governed more by a desire for some degree of urban continuity than by any intrinsic architectural quality, and in reality the scheme may well have benefited from a new design.

Behind the retained façade, Derek Tynan has fitted out the commercial shell as new design studios for fashion designer John Rocha. Using the cool minimalist language of the modern art gallery, a complex of interlocking double-height spaces and overlapping planes has been fashioned with a minimum of detail elaboration.

The red-brick front elevation sits comfortably within the street context. In contrast, the raised entrance court is a modernist world of white render, black steel windows and metalwork, and zinc cladding. The

Temple Bar

**Group 91 (Derek Tynan Architects) 1994**

**Temple Bar**

**Group 91 (Derek Tynan Architects) 1994**

design of the flats is carefully controlled to maintain privacy but let in sun and light (via complex sectional manoeuvring), especially in the duplex flats which have double-height living spaces.

The scheme demonstrates very clearly the feasibility – and, indeed, desirability – of living in the heart of the city, and how even the tightest and most unpromising sites can be turned to advantage with imagination and skill.

ADDRESS 25 Essex Street, 26–27 Essex Street East, 12–13 Temple Lane, Dublin 2
CLIENT Temple Bar Properties
STRUCTURAL ENGINEER Thorburn Colquhoun
COST IR£850,000
BUS/TRAIN City Centre
ACCESS none

**Group 91 (Derek Tynan Architects) 1994**

Temple Bar

**Group 91 (Derek Tynan Architects) 1994**

**The Granary Apartments**

While it is the buildings adjacent to this scheme – the Curved Street and 'The Ark' Children's Cultural Centre – that grab the attention, urban renewal also relies on quieter but nevertheless significant projects. The general grain of the Temple Bar area, and much of its charm and character, are created by the remaining nineteenth-century fabric, particularly the brick warehouses. In addition, they offer the potential for that most desirable of late twentieth-century urban residential models, the 'loft', of which The Granary is Dublin's first example.

Two old warehouse structures have been carefully renovated with large open-plan living spaces, allowing the original structure and volumes to remain largely uncompromised. In all there are six new flats, topped by a communal roof terrace commanding superb views over the area. The terrace is kitted out with a shady pergola and external fireplace, making it a true outdoor room. At ground level is a modest shop unit.

The warehouse character has been carefully maintained, with the old loading bays retained as external shutters and various hoists and industrial relics left *in situ*. The result is low key, but the Granary Apartments, and other similar schemes, provide the essential backdrop against which the architectural set pieces can shine.

**Temple Bar**

ADDRESS 20 Temple Lane, Temple Bar, Dublin 2
CLIENT Temple Bar Properties
STRUCTURAL ENGINEER O'Connor Sutton Cronin
BUS/TRAIN City Centre
ACCESS none

**Peter Twamley 1995**

# Arthouse Multimedia Centre for the Arts

The new Curved Street breaches the urban block between Temple Lane South and Eustace Street, allowing the east–west route to connect to Meeting House Square. The two new buildings which form the street, although related, are in fact by different architects. On the south side, the multimedia centre, set up to explore the potential of the computer in the arts, claims to be the first of its kind in the world. Its public facilities include a basement performance space (beneath the road itself), exhibition areas, a computer-based library and Cyberia, the internet café. In common with most of Temple Bar, the building is a combination of new and existing construction.

Arthouse and the Music Centre opposite (see page 176) have clearly been designed with considerable co-operation between their respective architects, who have used a common palette of materials and forms to create a piece of 1930s modern with more than a dash of Le Corbusier. Gone are the days when the principal complaint about modern architecture was that urban buildings ignored their context. These buildings may wear the clothes of the International Style, but they mesh with their surroundings, following the street line, parapet heights, and the scale and grain of the area to form an exemplary piece of urbanism.

The end elevations of the two buildings respond to the tall proportions of their common plot width with wall openings of an equally compatible scale. The street itself is more unified and horizontal, with large and small glazed openings scattered across the façades. The two entrances face each other at the centre of the street. Above these are large glazed openings in the form of large warehouse-style sliding screens which, when open, allow interaction between the buildings and the street. Arthouse is also fitted with a lifting beam – both a functional element and a contextual

**Group 91 (Shay Cleary Architects) 1995**

**Group 91 (Shay Cleary Architects) 1995**

reference. Rails have been fitted around the edges of the building to take event lighting, banners and a canvas roof which extends over the street.

Arthouse declares its purpose with banks of video screens on either side of the entrance, further extending interaction with the street. The large windows over the entrance suggest a correspondingly large atrium space inside, an expectation initially frustrated by entry into a narrow entrance hall with a low ceiling. Ahead is the information counter and a glass panorama lift, again raising expectations of a major internal space. To the right lies an exhibition area; to the left are the stairs down to the basement studio space and production unit (recently host to an orchestral performance in which each musician was in a different country).

The route to the first floor is architecturally more eventful, with a metal bridge and stair in front of the double-height shop window. The stair void is populated by another of Shay Cleary's handsome Meier-inspired free-form pillboxes (see also page 126). These stairs lead to the illusive atrium, the space around which the life of the building revolves, and home to the café and its array of Internet computers. The dynamic space rises through three storeys to a glass roof, where steel stairs and bridges connect the two halves of the building and offer an excellent vantage point for the contemplation of this successful urban intervention.

**Temple Bar**

ADDRESS Curved Street, Temple Bar, Dublin 2
CLIENT Temple Bar Properties
STRUCTURAL ENGINEER Thorburn Colquhoun
BUS/TRAIN City Centre
ACCESS Monday to Friday 10.00–17.30

**Group 91 (Shay Cleary Architects) 1995**

Temple Bar

**Group 91 (Shay Cleary Architects) 1995**

# Temple Bar Music Centre

The northern half of the new Curved Street, and complementary to the Arthouse opposite (see page 172), is the Music Centre, a grouping of semi-autonomous companies united by music interests. It was conceived as a centre for the hugely successful and profitable Irish music industry – Ireland is home to, among many others, U2, Van Morrison and Sinéad O'Connor – and to facilitate the next generation of musical plutocrats. The building combines recording studios in the basement, MusicBase (an information centre) on the first and second floors, and a music school on the third. The ground floor houses The Venue, a 340-seat performance space, and a café/bar. This complex mix of uses is housed within an equally complex mix of new and existing construction, with the plan having to untangle a brief which called for separate entrances and spaces but also allowed for the possibility of interaction and flexibility between them. The new Curved Street elevation provides the focus of the grouping and locates the various entrances, but large parts of the complex shelter behind the retained façades of the warehouses to 10 and 11 Temple Lane.

The main frontage shares the materials and forms of Arthouse to create the major urban set piece of the new street, arranging the parts into a graceful convex curve with a large glazed opening of steel windows and clear and opaque glazing. The principal entrance is marked by a projecting balcony – relating to both its own large-scale sliding doors and those on the Arthouse façade opposite – and a vivid yellow wall which extends from the interior with an invitation to enter. The curved entrance wall declares itself to be a screen wall at the Temple Lane corner, where a dramatic slice reveals a top-lit staircase forming one of the secondary entrances. The theme of screen façades around individual objects and set pieces runs throughout the building. The largest element to be treated in this way is the main auditorium, a three-storey acoustically insulated box

**Group 91 (McCullough and Mulvin Architects) 1996**

Temple Bar

**Group 91 (McCullough and Mulvin Architects) 1996**

clad in black steel louvres. This box sits behind the main elevation and the Temple Lane façades and is partially visible through the windows as well as creating a strong presence within the internal spaces. This architectural game is clearest at night when lighting highlights the 'box', but the effect is rather lost during the day when the black of the louvres recedes into the shadows.

Much is promised by the main entrance, where a yellow wall leads to a long, wide ramp which plunges down into the shadowy bowels of the building. The powerful axis, however, leads only to an escape stair and a narrow acoustic lobby giving entry to the auditorium. Access to the venue is, in fact, through the café at the front. Above the entrance a double-height space, facing the Curved Street on one side and a central courtyard on the other, allows further glimpses of the louvred auditorium box from the street.

ADDRESS Curved Street North, Temple Bar, Dublin 2
CLIENT Temple Bar Properties
STRUCTURAL ENGINEER Ove Arup and Partners
COST IR£2.5 million
BUS/TRAIN City Centre
ACCESS Monday to Friday 10.00–17.30, and for performances

**Temple Bar**

**Group 91 (McCullough and Mulvin Architects) 1996**

**Temple Bar**

**Group 91 (McCullough and Mulvin Architects) 1996**

# 'The Ark' Children's Cultural Centre

'The Ark' is a centre for children's activities, principally performance. From Eustace Street you appear to be entering a restoration of the Georgian Presbyterian Meeting House, only to have your expectations confounded as the building undergoes a surprising transformation into a full-blooded modern interior. Only the façade of the old Meeting House has been retained, supported from within by a concrete frame. The full width of the old building forms a double-height 'front of house' to a semi-circular amphitheatre which makes up the depth of the building. Stairs at one end of the foyer lead down to a dining area with a long refectory table for children's parties, covered by a part ceiling/part artwork of eroding metal and glass. Above the auditorium on the top floor, best reached by the lift, is a multipurpose space for arts and crafts, divided by an ingenious system of sliding walls and doors. This floor is placed above the top of the old front wall and set back to reduce the impact from the street. This is no weak mansard device, however, but a dramatic wriggling wall of 'look, no hands' glass, complete with *de rigueur* Group 91 saw-tooth monitor rooflights extending back into the space.

The interiors are architecture in the raw, with all materials left unfinished and in their natural state: rough concrete, timber, galvanised steel, old brick. This gives them a generous, robust warmth and solidity (the antithesis of the fragile 'designer interior') and makes them ideal play spaces for children. The auditorium is child-sized, with simple bleacher seating and a balcony. Walls are lined with perforated hardboard to allow Polaroid photographs to be pegged up. On arrival, visiting children are armed with a camera, and the walls are quickly filling up with a rogues' gallery of mug shots. Other inventive ideas abound, such as child-height windows up on the balcony. The most dramatic feature, however, is the way in which the whole rear of the stage opens up, via a spectacular verti-

**Temple Bar**

**Group 91 (Shane O'Toole and Michael Kelly) 1995**

**Group 91 (Shane O'Toole and Michael Kelly) 1995**

cally-folding wall to a design by Santiago Calatrava. When open, the wall reveals Meeting House Square behind, allowing the stage to be used for both outdoor and 'in the round' performances.

The new façade to Meeting House Square is in the same soft red brick as the adjacent Photography Centre (see page 184), with the saw-tooth lights forming a distinctive roofline. A bellows-like projecting bay houses the stage, and its pre-patinated copper forms an external proscenium arch. The inventive detail continues externally with a black granite corner buffer straight out of Berlage's Amsterdam Stock Exchange. But, despite the sophistication on display, the elevation retains a simplicity not unlike that of a child's drawing, and speaks eloquently of the use within.

The practice of retaining old façades in new constructions has many detractors, who feel it devalues the integrity of the new work and is merely a sop to the conservation lobby. 'The Ark' emphatically contradicts this position by using a fine old façade to create dialogue with the new work, both enriching the architectural experience and providing continuity within the renewal processes that constitute a living city. For those who still feel that a new building should have a new façade, then 'The Ark' obliges with its Meeting House Square frontage.

ADDRESS 11A Eustace Street, Temple Bar, Dublin 2
CLIENT Temple Bar Properties
STRUCTURAL ENGINEER KML
COST IR£2.4 million
BUS/TRAIN City Centre
ACCESS open

**Temple Bar**

**Group 91 (Shane O'Toole and Michael Kelly) 1995**

Temple Bar

Group 91 (Shane O'Toole and Michael Kelly) 1995

# National Photography Centre and Gallery of Photography

Monumentality is not exclusive to the large scale, as John Tuomey's early mentor James Stirling often pointed out. Temple Bar's most monumental new building, the new National Photography Centre, proves the point. Approached from Essex Street East, its hot red brick and hunky form are almost overpowering, its low, arched entrance seemingly compressed by the weight of the construction above. The walls rise sheer from the street, and there is no stepping or other conventional allowance for the narrow passage into Meeting House Square. The deep-set strip windows, with squat circular columns and sculptured zinc-clad forms, all accentuate the massiveness of the wall and create a sense of Roman grandeur. Fragments of stone quoining scattered amongst the brick and the suppression of conventional detailing such as window sills, reinforce the illusion of something more ancient.

The centre is split into two separate parts: a red-brick building housing the photographic archive of the National Gallery and a school of photography and, across Meeting House Square, the Gallery of Photography. The latter, an equally enigmatic object building clad in Portland stone, hides the flank wall of the earlier Irish Film Centre (also by O'Donnell and Tuomey, see page 194). The buildings on either side of the square are linked, appropriately, by light: movies can be shown outdoors by projecting them from the photography centre on to the gallery opposite (where the large central window acts as a screen).

At first glance the architectural forms appear to have been chosen quite arbitrarily, but they are in fact part of a personal vocabulary developed by architects with a particular interest in the psychological impact and metaphorical use of form. For instance, the nicks out of the right corner of the gallery façade refer to the sprocket holes in film, and the wedge

**Group 91 (O'Donnell and Tuomey Architects) 1996**

**Temple Bar**

**Group 91 (O'Donnell and Tuomey Architects) 1996**

form of the ground-floor window refers to the journey from light to dark experienced in a photographic darkroom or the cinema. The use of a highly personalised language, however, is open to misinterpretation – here the gallery elevations suggest, erroneously, the presence of a raked floor auditorium within.

The upper floors of the Photography Centre house the DIT School of Photography and its collection of darkrooms, studios and teaching spaces. These uses presented O'Donnell and Tuomey with a fundamental contradiction – between the architectural desire for light and openings, and the client requirement for darkness (for both photographic work and archive storage). This conflict has been resolved by making openings in the external walls and filling them with zinc cladding. On the main building, the major openings at roof level indicate the location of the photographic studios; but here, at least, lightweight infill panels offer the possibility of window installation at a later date.

Across the square the gallery contains space for photographic exhibitions and allied lecture and workshop events. Entry is from the side, at the high point of the wedge window leading into a ground-floor bookshop. The main gallery is above, reached via an opaque-glass stair tower. It is a double-height space, announced on the main elevation by the large window that doubles as the external projection screen. The main room has a complex section with concealed rooflights and folding exhibition panels; balcony spaces with small rooms provide a variety of hanging possibilities. The stair continues upwards to a roof terrace, from where there are views down to the square.

The small but elegant granite-clad façade adjacent to the gallery entrance links the square and the new buildings to the complex sequence of spaces of the Irish Film Centre next door, thus extending further the

**Group 91 (O'Donnell and Tuomey Architects) 1996**

richness of the townscape experience. This richness, which makes up the very essence of the city, is evident too in the difference between these two buildings from the same architects – a difference noted by the gallery's bookshop manager who, on meeting John Tuomey at the opening, proceeded to congratulate him on the excellent gallery and to express his relief that they hadn't ended up with the architects of the archive building across the square. Tuomey's reply is not recorded.

**Temple Bar**

ADDRESS Meeting House Square, Temple Bar, Dublin 2
CLIENT Temple Bar Properties
STRUCTURAL ENGINEER Muir Associates
COST IR£2.4 million
BUS/TRAIN City Centre
ACCESS open

**Group 91 (O'Donnell and Tuomey Architects) 1996**

Temple Bar

**Group 91 (O'Donnell and Tuomey Architects) 1996**

# Meeting House Square and Mixed-Use Building

Meeting House Square, the second major new external space on the east-west route through Temple Bar, is surrounded on all sides by new cultural centres; 'The Ark' Children's Centre (page 180), the National Photography Centre and the Gallery of Photography (page 184) all interact directly with it. (The theatre at 'The Ark' has an external proscenium arch, and the Photography Centre has a zinc-clad projection box with a corresponding external screen on the gallery façade for alfresco movies.) The east side is formed by two new mixed-use buildings, with a café and shops opening on to the square.

It is intended that the east–west route should run from the Curved Street, through the new opening adjacent to 'The Ark', and then be deflected southwards by the square to meet Essex Street East. Here a new pedestrian route – the Poddle Bridge – was planned across the river, but regrettably this is not now to be realised. A lesser route continues west from the square to connect to the Olympia Theatre and Project Arts Centre. This major grouping forms a cultural hot-spot which it is hoped will populate the square with street theatre and other Beaubourg-style events. It also forms an architectural head-to-head, with any potential unity of design sacrificed on the altar of self-expression.

Paul Keogh, the architect responsible for both the planning of the square and the mixed-use building, had been in the vanguard of the regionalist tendency of the 1980s. In many ways, of all his contemporaries he came the closest to capturing the spirit of an Irish classicism in a series of small, Aldo Rossi-inspired projects. Even his largest project to date, the Charlesland Golf Club (see page 282), is governed by the same simple rationalism, particularly in plan. This mixed-use building, however, illustrates a surprising change of style, but its more conventional 'new

Temple Bar

**Group 91 (Paul Keogh) 1995**

Temple Bar

**Group 91 (Paul Keogh) 1995**

modern' idiom has neither the conviction of O'Donnell and Tuomey's personalised style nor the bravura of Shane O'Toole's Children's Theatre. The building form is fragmented by the site. The shop building, cut off from the main block by the square's west exit, becomes an extension to the earlier Film Centre library and is carried out in complementary manner. The northern end of the main building is formed by a small existing building, refaced on the square exit side. Between the two, the new building has to resolve the changes in scale, the differing geometries and the urban significance of street and square, and a complex mix of internal spaces – in other words, it needs to be a strong, simple structure in the Keogh tradition. Drawings published prior to construction showed just such a building – complete with loggias on to the square and at roof level. A late change of plan, however, resulted in an increase in accommodation but a loss of clarity. Nevertheless, the double-height restaurant with a glazed wall to the square is a fine space which will animate the area. At high level, a butterfly roof and central window signal a significant internal space occupied by the Gaiety School of Acting.

The square itself is simply carried out in granite paving, with a central circular pattern acknowledging the varying axes of the space.

ADDRESS Meeting House Square West, Temple Bar, Dublin 2
CLIENT Temple Bar Properties
STRUCTURAL ENGINEER Muir Associates
COST IR£917,000
BUS/TRAIN City Centre
ACCESS public areas only

**Temple Bar**

**Group 91 (Paul Keogh) 1995**

Temple Bar

**Group 91 (Paul Keogh) 1995**

# Irish Film Centre

The Irish Film Centre was the model for the Temple Bar project, conceived and built before the Structure Plan was even a twinkle in Charlie Haughey's eye. By the time the plan was mooted, the Film Centre was already a living, breathing example of the Group 91 approach to urban regeneration and renewal. It thus played an important part in the decision to allow a group of largely unbuilt architects to participate in the original competition. The Film Centre layout even foresaw the creation of Meeting House Square, long before there was any possibility that it would become a reality.

O'Donnell and Tuomey had been trying to build the Film Centre since 1985, and had prepared schemes for various locations before the present site was purchased from the Quakers, who had acquired a diverse collection of buildings over many years. The existing buildings presented various pros and cons: although the two cinemas would fit neatly into existing spaces, the accommodation was stranded in the middle of an urban block with no main, street elevation. But, ultimately, these severe constraints have been turned to skilful advantage in a *tour de force* of 'townscape' design.

The scheme represents a casebook study of Gordon Cullen's original 'Townscape' thesis. The entrance from Eustace Street, marked by a neon sign, is a narrow tunnel leading to a larger, brighter space just visible at the end. This sets up a 'here and there' relationship, encouraging anticipation and exploration. Reinforcing this impression is the glass floor (metaphorically intended as a reel of film) which links the entrance to the central space. The barrel-vaulted passage leads to the principal central courtyard, whose main façade is concealed until arrival. For film-goers, this is where the ticket office, cinema entry, bar, restaurant and shop are situated. The glass-roofed space has an external character, with a new

**O'Donnell and Tuomey Architects 1992**

**Temple Bar**

**O'Donnell and Tuomey Architects 1992**

'façade' reminiscent, appropriately, of a film set. Entry to the main cinema is behind a blue-rendered wall.

For those using the centre as a short cut through the block, a door in the shop provides access to the other side. This door opens on to a tall, narrow colonnade leading to Meeting House Square. A change in level emphasises the contrast between the dark enclosure of the arcade and the bright openness of the square, and also gives a high-level view of the square on entry. Alternatively, by passing between the columns of the arcade you reach a small courtyard outside the new film archive building and library. From here, steps lead down to Sycamore Street, although progression is compromised by a narrow security gate at the bottom.

Once in the square, a look back reveals a mannered façade clad in limestone. Through the windows of the projection room, the flickering light of the projector adds a poetic touch of drama to the night-time view.

The spatial intricacy and variety of this architectural promenade are complemented every step of the way by a material dialogue between old and new; stylish – indeed, stylised – detailing; and the warmth of naturally finished materials and textures.

**Temple Bar**

ADDRESS Eustace Street, Temple Bar, Dublin 2
CLIENT Irish Film Centre Ltd
STRUCTURAL ENGINEER Fearon O'Neill Rooney
COST IR£1.8 million
BUS/TRAIN City Centre
ACCESS open daily, 11.00–24.00

**O'Donnell and Tuomey Architects 1992**

**O'Donnell and Tuomey Architects 1992**

# DESIGNyard Applied Arts Centre

The arts centre is housed in a converted eighteenth-century china ware-house. Externally, the carefully restored tuck-pointed brickwork sets it apart from other brick buildings in the street, and equal care has been shown internally, with reinstated cast-iron columns and rooms planned to respect the original structure and layout. Entry is through a newly created arcade, behind which lies a glass shop window, protected from the street by the narrow arcade openings. At night these are closed off with new gates designed by Kathy Prendergast, based on city plans.

Internally, the eye is immediately drawn to the floor, where a mosaic pattern (representing the River Poddle which flows below the building) winds its way through the ground-floor Jewellery Gallery. This is formed by the existing space of the old building and has low-key glass display cases. To the rear of the gallery a former yard has been roofed over with a tent of fabric to provide space for the spiral stair, allowing it to avoid impacting on the old structure.

The upstairs furniture gallery, occupying the floor plate of the old building, is one of the best places in town for contemporary Irish designs.

On many levels this is a textbook example of contemporary restoration, though perhaps somewhat chilly in character due to the old and new showing each other respect rather than empathy.

ADDRESS 12 Essex Street East, Temple Bar, Dublin 2
CLIENT Temple Bar Properties
STRUCTURAL ENGINEER Thomas Garland and Partners
COST IR£500,000
BUS/TRAIN City Centre
ACCESS Monday to Saturday 10.30–17.30

**Temple Bar**

**Felim Dunne and Associates with Robinson Keefe and Devane 1994**

**Felim Dunne and Associates with Robinson Keefe and Devane 1994**

# The Kitchen Nightclub

This is the coolest nightclub in Dublin, not least because it is owned by the rock band U2. Its design is based, according to the architect, on the feel of a 1950s butcher's shop: terrazzo floors, spiky stainless steel details, beech worktops, and sculptured free-form walls and ceilings apparently made from a 'soft, cheese-like substance'.

A strong hint of what is to come is given by the leather-clad entrance lobby, encountered before descending the stairs to a surreal subterranean world where Dali meets Peter Greenaway. Here the floor slopes away, the walls curve, the ceiling dips and dives – even before any alcohol has been taken! Kitsch *Twin Peaks*-style suede curtains drape the walls of myriad little alcoves and inlets, and the 10-metre-long bar has blue fibre optics to make your drink glow as if radioactive. A moat surrounds a dance floor equipped with a sound system capable of delivering music at a mind-expanding 128 decibels. Complex acoustic separation from the Clarence Hotel above involves layers of mineral wool insulation and a thick layer of lead, making it the place to be in Dublin if ever a nuclear bomb is dropped.

ADDRESS Clarence Hotel, Temple Bar, Dublin 2
CLIENT U2
COST IR£300,000
BUS/TRAIN City Centre
ACCESS evenings

Temple Bar

**Ross Cahill-O'Brien and Associates Ltd 1994**

Temple Bar

**Ross Cahill-O'Brien and Associates Ltd 1994**

# The Porter House Bar

Given the central role of the public house in the life of Dubliners, we were hoping to find at least one good modern bar interior. This isn't it, but it does have its moments. The Porter House is one of that new breed of public house, the micro brewery, which brews its own beers on the premises and uses the process to 'theme' the design. Externally, the warehouse context of Temple Bar forms the aesthetic: through the windows of a glass and timber corner tower can be seen the equipment and paraphernalia of the brewing process, in particular the large copper piping that introduces the main motif of the design. Internally, the pub is deceptively large, with a series of half and quarter levels spiralling around a three-storey central atrium which succeeds in creating spatial drama and wide views without sacrificing the intimate scale essential to the bar's atmosphere. The detailing is often inventive – standard copper-plumbing door handles and rails, and back-lit glass display cases which dramatise the rough texture of the brickwork – and the extensive use of timber surfaces offers warmth and conviviality. This promising mix of elements, however, is let down by the furniture and balustrade design, both of which are ham-fisted and over-dominant.

The reinterpretation of the traditional spirit of the pub has been a continuing problem for modernism, with most new bars either cod traditional or package 'brasserie'. Maybe the Porter House is a stage-post along the way to a more satisfactory solution.

ADDRESS Corner of Essex Street East and Parliament Street, Temple Bar, Dublin 2
STRUCTURAL ENGINEER Stanislaus, Kenny & Partners
BUS/TRAIN City Centre
ACCESS open

**Temple Bar**

**Frank Ennis & Associates 1996**

**Frank Ennis & Associates 1996**

# Viking Centre

Following the east–west route of Temple Bar along Essex Street West, one's attention is drawn to an enigmatic grouping of buildings linked by an elegant steel bridge. Below this is a panel engraved with significant-looking cosmic markings. A closer inspection reveals that this relief sculpture (by Grace Weir) is on the rear of the Viking Museum. Entry is, in fact, from Lower Exchange Street, the whole museum being a shot-gun marriage of five separate buildings whose only connection is that they were built next to each other. The group consists of a church, presbytery and a former boys' school facing Exchange Street, and a girls' school facing Essex Street with a two-storey slope across the site as the ground falls down to the Liffey. The group of buildings lies close to Woodquay (see page 208), the site of the original Viking town.

Entry to the museum is via the steel-and-glass link between the boys' school and the church. Radical surgery has been required to make sense of this disparate group, particularly on the boys' school where the interior has been completely removed to allow a new ramp to spiral round the edges. The entrance sequence of installations around the ramp is intended to transport the visitor back to a time when rape and pillage were not what traffic engineers did to old cities. When fully regressed, the visitor enters a new mezzanine level within the old church, the fabric of which has been skilfully restored. Above its elaborate ceiling is an entirely new steel structure, to which it is stitched. The gaps at the cornice both honestly reveal the new changes and allow smoke extraction. To the south, the gothic windows are replicas, made of timber and painted, rather less honestly, to look like the original stone. This room demonstrates the rationale of the work – partially complete or damaged original work is seamlessly restored, while entirely new elements are clearly expressed as contemporary insertions.

**Gilroy McMahon Architects 1996**

Temple Bar

The circulation route moves from the church into a glazed bridge (an exemplar of structural clarity and spare detailing), and then into the top floor of the former girls' school. Here an enfilade of rooms has been formed through the cross-walls of the original building, with new roof trusses made from old pine to match any existing ones. Glass blocks and circular rooflights distinguish the new elements. The axially positioned stair takes visitors down to the final space of the museum – the 'black box' – where the museum's most precious object, a Viking ship, is displayed.

Externally, the new construction is best seen from the courtyard, where the impeccable steelwork is combined with cedar boarding and the glass-reinforced-concrete-panelled sculptural relief to subtle effect.

Somewhat against the odds, the architects have managed to wrestle a coherent sequence of spaces out of this oddball group. What, in the end, is experienced as variety could so easily have been either a series of disjunctive collisions or unity at the expense of the differing internal characters. Although what has been achieved is no mean architectural feat, one suspects that the museum – and other cultural institutions within conversions around Dublin – is a marriage of convenience between use and building.

ADDRESS Lower Exchange Street, Dublin 2
CLIENT Temple Bar Properties/Dublin Tourism
STRUCTURAL ENGINEER Horgan Lynch and Partners
COST IR£5.5 million
ACCESS open

**Temple Bar**

**Gilroy McMahon Architects 1996**

**Gilroy McMahon Architects 1996**

**Civic Offices**

Sites in Dublin do not come more controversial than this one. In 1974 Woodquay was the most important archaeological site in Ireland, marking the centre of the original Viking settlement. It was also the site chosen by Dublin Corporation for its new Civic Offices, designed by Sam Stephenson, an architect with a portfolio of Dublin's most controversial modern buildings. The Corporation and the conservation lobby locked horns in the mother of all environmental battles, which eventually reached a temporary lull following the construction of phase 1 – the twin octagonal towers (the infamous 'bunkers') at the end of Dame Street. The threat of the completed scheme (including a further two matching towers) hovered over the city like a dark cloud for years until, in 1992, an architectural competition for the phase 2 buildings was won by Scott Tallon Walker.

The new building had complex urban problems to solve: the site, at a significant bend in the Liffey amid the jumble of the quays, is surrounded by some of Dublin's finest monuments; the townscape damage of the Civic Offices had to be repaired, and the Temple Bar east-west pedestrian route concluded. Also, much of the site behind the quays frontage had to be kept clear of construction to allow for future archaeological digs.

The building houses various council departments, including the architects and planners, and is divided into two parallel blocks – five storeys on the quays, rising to six behind. The gap is filled with a full-height atrium, and a second complementary atrium is placed between the two original towers. A two-storey link bridges the pedestrian street which extends from Temple Bar. A new entrance off the quays, marked by a well-positioned large-scale sculpture by Michael Warren, links through to another off Christchurch Place between the original towers, creating a pedestrian route through the site, enlivened by the new atrium spaces.

**Temple Bar**

**Scott Tallon Walker Architects 1994**

The scale of the building and the use of immaculately resolved Wicklow-granite cladding marks it out as a new civic 'monument' on the quays. The top-level balcony forms a minimal cornice which extends at either end to make a porch over the entrance and a sharp prow to frame views of the cathedral from O'Donovan Rossa Bridge. To the south, extensive sun-screening to the windows is part of an important energy-saving strategy which uses the central atrium to regulate heating and ventilation to the office spaces.

Behind the building, the landscaped park comes as a surprise, allowing open views of the cathedral ridge and terminating the east–west link with an open-air amphitheatre. Meanwhile, behind it all, the stubborn 'bunkers' wear their polite new clothing with about as much grace as Mike Tyson would wear a tutu.

**Temple Bar**

ADDRESS Woodquay, Dublin 2
CLIENT Dublin Corporation
STRUCTURAL ENGINEER Ove Arup and Partners
COST IR£18 million
BUS 51, 51B, 70, 70X
ACCESS open

**Scott Tallon Walker Architects 1994**

**Scott Tallon Walker Architects 1994**

# Trinity College

# Dining Hall and Atrium

Of the architects at the heart of the regionalist debate of the 1980s, de Blacam and Meagher and Paul Keogh probably came closest to defining the elusive spirit of an Irish architectural character – and, in Dublin, the Trinity College Dining Hall is the clearest manifestation of this quality.

Facing out into the main quad, the dining hall was an essential part of the eighteenth-century college, although surrounded by 300 years of accumulated construction. De Blacam and Meagher were in the process of drawing up plans for the rationalisation of this dense mass when a fire destroyed the interiors in July 1984. The buildings today are a combination of carefully restored classical interiors and new construction and adaption. In the dining hall itself, new refectory furniture has been designed by the architects following the eighteenth-century model. Fragments of the mouldings and profiles which survived the fire enabled much of the original work to be reconstructed. This painstaking task served as a useful masterclass in Georgian craftsmanship, which the architects have assimilated and reinterpreted to great effect in those areas where accurate reconstruction was less critical.

Sense has been made of the dense muddle of construction by sinking a bold atrium space into the deep plan adjacent to the dining hall, allowing the new arrangement of kitchens, serveries, bars and student society rooms to revolve around it. The space itself occupies the full height of the building, from the basement to the newly exposed eighteenth-century roof trusses of the old kitchen. For such an important space the route from the side entrance is somewhat convoluted, but this also heightens the sense of discovery as the low-ceilinged basement areas give way to the top-lit four-storey volume. The atrium is lined in oak cladding, with balustraded balconies or opening shutters providing the occupants of the rooms behind with a choice of privacy or interaction with the main space.

**de Blacam and Meagher Architects 1986**

Trinity College

**de Blacam and Meagher Architects 1986**

Wearing the influence of Louis Kahn on its sleeve, the space manages to be true to a contemporary spirit yet coexist happily with its historic surroundings, a balancing act successfully achieved by all the new elements and details throughout the building.

Around the atrium, various social spaces – the Buttery Bar in the vaulted undercroft below the dining room, the serveries and the dining rooms – share an understated vocabulary. With solid oak, stone details, timber wainscoting and diamond-pattern tiled floors, they are reminiscent of below-stairs domestic areas in large country houses. Careful symmetrical arrangements and simple, solid oak furniture extend this appropriate analogy.

Hidden away on the first floor is a further gem: the Senior Common Room Bar, built as a recreation of Adolf Loos' famous Viennese Kärtner Bar of 1907. The small, dark, smoky room has an authentic feel, despite the painted-MDF 'marble' ceiling slabs and a mysteriously handed layout. But why rebuild a modern classic? There is a certain similarity between the beam-and-column structure of the bar's mirrored colonnade and the structure of the atrium, but maybe it was the literal result of Loos' own arguments in favour of following established topologies. Or maybe it's just such a good space that every city should have one.

ADDRESS Trinity College, Dublin 2
STRUCTURAL ENGINEER Ove Arup and Partners
COST IR£4 million
BUS City Centre; DART Pearse Station
ACCESS by arrangement with the Buildings Office

**de Blacam and Meagher Architects 1986**

Trinity College

**Trinity College**

de Blacam and Meagher Architects 1986

**Beckett Theatre**

The format of the Trinity campus places great emphasis on the narrow routes, at the quadrangle corners, which interconnect the external spaces. Passing through the last of these routes, known as 'The Narrows', at the point where the enclosed squares open out into the playing fields to the east, a large, skilfully positioned oak-clad tower suddenly reveals itself to dramatise the confinement of the route. Closer inspection identifies the structure as the public front of the new Beckett Theatre for the Drama Studies faculty. The complex consists of the theatre itself (a 'black box' auditorium), a smaller Players Theatre, a Dance Studio, and associated front- and back-of-house facilities.

The problem of what to do with the large and inexpressive blank box of the main auditorium has been solved by burying the volume into the depth of the building fabric. The west and east elevations are obscured by adjacent buildings, and the north elevation to Pearse Street is formed by a strip of existing buildings which have been converted to offices and classrooms. As a secondary function, they form an acoustic buffer zone between the auditorium and the traffic noise of Pearse Street.

The remainder of the accommodation is piled up into the timber tower that announces the presence of this hidden complex. Chunky timber columns form an arcade at ground level and lead to the main entrance and box office. The front-of-house facilities occupy the remainder of the ground floor. Stacked above is the small Players Theatre in a double-height space, and above that the Dance Studio occupies a square top-lit space with an intricate, steel roof structure. The tower is, in fact, a steel-framed structure clad in oak framing and panelling, a fact revealed within the arcade space where the construction is clearly expressed. The second- and third-floor levels are articulated by outward steps in the cladding, allowing rainwater to be thrown clear of the façade. The tower is topped

**de Blacam and Meagher Architects 1993**

**de Blacam and Meagher Architects 1993**

by a hat-like, pitched slate roof, with its wide brim forming a generous overhanging eaves.

There is a strong family connection between the tower and de Blacam and Meagher's earlier atrium in the college dining rooms (see page 214), with timber framing and panelling with large opening shutters forming a shared vocabulary. It is almost as if the new tower represents the solid, 'positive' equivalent of the atrium's 'negative' void.

The tower also illustrates the architects' on-going preoccupation with the work of Louis Kahn (Shane de Blacam worked in Kahn's office for three years during the early part of his career). In this instance it is Kahn's Fisher House that springs to mind. His influence is apparent in the crisply detailed timber cladding, the window openings, and the use of a clear geometric form to resolve an awkward contextual jumble. For some observers, the use of timber recalls Elizabethan playhouses; others see a connection to the work of Aldo Rossi, in particular his floating theatre. Certainly it is a building rich in references and allusions, one of the most subtle being the parallel between the silver-grey of its oak cladding and the Wicklow granite of the surrounding buildings – a connection which will strengthen as the building matures.

ADDRESS Trinity College, Dublin 2
STRUCTURAL ENGINEER Ove Arup and Partners
COST IR£2 million
BUS City Centre; DART Pearse Station
ACCESS none

**Trinity College**

**de Blacam and Meagher Architects 1993**

# Student Housing

Adjacent to the Beckett Theatre a small development houses 100 student rooms in two parallel four-storey blocks perpendicular to the perimeter terrace fronting Pearse Street. Ground-floor circulation runs laterally through the centre of the blocks and across the narrow courtyard between them. This allows for a phased development (two further blocks are planned) but each phase is complete in itself – an interesting alternative to a spine building where the form, in a sense, is never completed.

Entry is from an octagonal space at the centre of each block, with stairs at the north and south rising to the central corridors of the upper floors. The octagonal form of the entry space is a mini version of the main entry to the college from College Green. The whole layout has a satisfactory simplicity, with low-pitch roofs running to deep overhanging eaves giving a feel of Frank Lloyd Wright. The paired block-end elevations facing on to the playing fields have blank walls at ground- and first-floor levels. A low-level block to the south, again windowless, links the two blocks and acknowledges the pedestrian route across the front, making a visual plinth. For the most part, materials are natural and self-finished: unsealed hardwood windows; slate roofs with lead-roll hips. The walls, originally self-finished grey render, have recently been painted cream, thus destroying the continuity between fair-faced materials, particularly affecting the window/wall relationship.

ADDRESS Trinity College, Dublin 2
STRUCTURAL ENGINEER Ove Arup and Partners
COST IR£1.5 million
DART Pearse Station
ACCESS none

**de Blacam and Meagher Architects 1990**

Trinity College

**de Blacam and Meagher Architects 1990**

# O'Reilly Institute for Communications and Technology

At its north-eastern corner the close-knit infrastructure of Trinity College starts to break down. The high-level railway from Pearse Station cuts a corner out of the site at a point where, ideally, the enclosure of the campus needs to be reinforced. Prior to the construction of the O'Reilly Institute, Westland Row, a grand Georgian terrace which forms the eastern boundary of the college, was unceremoniously truncated by the railway. Behind it was an untidy collection of rear extensions and small buildings along College Lane. The construction of the new institute offered an opportunity to heal this wound and remake the back areas of the college.

The institute was the first part of a structure plan for the area, since extended by the Biotechnology Building. It contains an Innovation Centre, the Computer Science Department and the main college computer, and Physics Research Laboratories. The site strategy aimed to link a three-storey deep-plan building to the existing Georgian terrace with a glass-roofed atrium concourse, thus forming a new eastern route within the college. The level differences and idiosyncrasies of the older buildings could then be absorbed by the atrium margin, using bridges and stairs within the atrium space. The main building is itself divided by a further glass-roofed courtyard which provides light into the deep plan. The buildings on Westland Row were either rebuilt as replicas or restored.

The basic strategy of the scheme, a variation of the familiar spine building, creates an expandable system which, diagrammatically at least, responds well to the form of the existing terrace. But however appropriate this diagram may be, a large building on a sensitive site requires further manipulation if it is to respond adequately to the contextual forces acting on it. The essential design problem in linear buildings – whether gothic cathedrals or one such as this – is how to conclude satisfactorily a building

**Scott Tallon Walker Architects 1988**

of potentially infinite length. Here, the end adjacent to the railway bridge shows no recognition of this issue; it makes no response to the bridge beyond a blank elevation for acoustic protection, giving the impression that it would continue northwards should the railway ever be demolished. The Westland Row terrace, however, stops short of the end of the new building and reveals the side elevation of the atrium. The main entrance is positioned here, reorientating the axis of the atrium and forming an entrance courtyard as a conclusion of sorts.

The elevations and construction of the building also contribute to a diagrammatic air. The steel portal frames of the atrium have a relentless rhythm which overpowers the potentially subtle relationship with the rear of the existing terrace. The elevations consist of an equally relentless grid of square, granite-aggregate GRC panels. Matching square windows finished flush with the panels preclude any potential for scale and articulation in the openings. On the other hand, the quality and consistency of the construction and the single-minded pursuit of the original idea demand a certain respect.

Internally the timber panelling and the quality of light have a softening effect, as does the banana tree in the courtyard. This has grown so vigorously that it has blocked the fire escape, but an ecologically sound decision was taken to install a new fire escape rather than chop it down.

ADDRESS Trinity College, Dublin 2
STRUCTURAL ENGINEER Joseph McCullough and Partners
COST IR£3.5 million
DART Pearse Station
ACCESS by appointment with College Secretary

**Scott Tallon Walker Architects 1988**

Trinity College

Trinity College

**Scott Tallon Walker Architects 1988**

# Rowan Hamilton Building and National Pharmaceutical Biotechnology Centre

The coarse-grained planning strategy of the O'Reilly Institute (page 224) is continued in the later phases of the eastern masterplan, providing accommodation for the Engineering Faculty and the Biotechnology Department. The block adjacent to the first phase is the William Rowan Hamilton Building, with a library stacked over two floors of lecture theatres and seminar rooms. Adjacent to this and completing this phase of the development is the National Pharmaceutical Biotechnology Centre.

The placing of the main circulation in the glazed spine puts the bulk of the new building between the spine and the main approach from the campus, creating a deep, narrow slot entrance between the institute and the Hamilton Building. By placing the main source of dynamic interest away from the face of the building, the architects have lost a means of enlivening the elevations. This has been partly addressed by a two-storey arcade with shops and a café, but the potential for a lively public space is somewhat reduced by the smoked black glazing and security restrictions on door openings. But the final phase of construction, connecting both the glazed spine and the arcade to Lincoln Place, should make sense of the planning logic and provide the necessary pedestrian movement to animate these currently dormant spaces.

ADDRESS Trinity College, Dublin 2
STRUCTURAL ENGINEER Lee McCullough and Partners
COST IR£5 million
DART Pearse Station
ACCESS by appointment with College Secretary

Trinity College

**Scott Tallon Walker Architects 1993**

**Trinity College**

**Scott Tallon Walker Architects 1993**

# Student Residences at Goldsmith Hall

The main event in this otherwise straightforward exercise is the new bridge link from the north-east corner of the Trinity College grounds. Entry from the college side is via a discreet door in the side of a free-standing stair and lift tower. Clothed in glass and grey limestone, the tower raises pedestrians up to a glazed bridge across Westland Row. The superstructure of the bridge is suspended from graceful steel arches which echo the curved roof of adjacent Pearse Station. The elegance of the new white structure is further emphasised by comparison with the gritty and chunky neighbouring rail bridge and viaduct which severs the corner off the Trinity campus at this point.

The housing itself is polite and well mannered, with a modern tendency held in check by classical undertones. The long façade to Pearse Street contrasts serried rows of windows (reflecting the repetitive internal room layout) with vertical glass oriel windows at the corners and over street entrances. Only a rash of shark's-teeth bay windows disturbs the symmetry and repose.

Trinity College

ADDRESS Corner of Pearse Street and Westland Row, Dublin 2
STRUCTURAL ENGINEER Ove Arup and Partners
COST IR£6.6 million
BUS 1, 3; DART Pearse Station
ACCESS none

**Murray O'Laoire Associates 1996**

**Murray O'Laoire Associates 1996**

**Arás an Phiarsaigh**

Another form of urban renewal with a long historical pedigree is the refacing of an older building. Although not a common occurrence in recent years, it has been adopted here as part of the rehabilitation of a 1970s office block. The original building was constructed with future road-widening in mind, with the angled relationship to its Georgian neighbour predicting (incorrectly) the ultimate destruction of the entire terrace in the name of city planning. Following the purchase of the building by Trinity College for the Business Studies Department, the architects were able to repair the damage resulting from this error of foresight by re-establishing the street line with a new triangular sliver of infill. The modern brick-clad form displays an affinity with the Georgian terrace it now completes. Its deep reveals and reticent detailing are reminiscent of recent work by de Blacam and Meagher (compare the Stack B offices, page 52). The entrance position has been reversed to open from the campus side into a serpentine concourse, with the street entrance played down and placed in the glazed overcladding which now covers the former office block.

The refacing of the building manages to repair a small but important discontinuity in the city fabric. It is not entirely a selfless gesture to urban design, however; the new section also provides a valuable 1900 square metres of 'nett lettable'.

ADDRESS Pearse Street, Dublin 2
STRUCTURAL ENGINEER John Doyle and Associates
COST IR£4 million
DART Pearse Station
ACCESS none

Trinity College

**Moloney O'Beirne Architects 1996**

**Moloney O'Beirne Architects 1996**

# Department of Mechanical Engineering

The classical Parsons Building is at the point where Lincoln Place angles into the corner of the Trinity campus. The new extension is designed to mediate between this building (housing the Department of Mechanical and Manufacturing Engineering) and the surrounding structures on the orthogonal grid of the campus. The resultant extension uses a granite-clad podium moulded by the contextual forces, surmounted by a cubic block which respects surrounding parapet heights. A ceremonial flight of steps runs up the side to the existing main entrance, avoiding trees to the right. A small side stair gives access to the podium roof terrace with its collection of monitor rooflights. The podium contains a workshop, and the upper block is filled with laboratories, seminar rooms and offices.

On the elevations, industrial details such as large sliding doors and lifting beams reflect the building's use, and a variety of materials – basalt cladding, aluminium windows, and panels with clear and obscure glass – adds richness.

The extension is a further example of a distinctly modern building on the Trinity campus settling with ease into its historic setting. The whole composition has a flavour of the work of Alvaro Siza, particularly in the way the inflections of the form not only make a contextual gesture but also add movement and fluidity to the building form.

ADDRESS Parsons Building, Trinity College, Dublin 2
STRUCTURAL ENGINEER Ove Arup and Partners
COST IR£1 million
DART Pearse Station
ACCESS none

**Trinity College**

**Grafton Architects 1996**

**Trinity College**

**Grafton Architects 1996**

**Dental Hospital**

Ahrends Burton and Koralek set up in practice together after winning the 1967 competition for the Berkeley Library at Trinity College (still one of Dublin's best modern buildings). This was followed by the Arts Buildings in 1980, and ABK is currently extending and refurbishing the Dental School in Lincoln Place. The work involves the renovation of the existing building fronting the street and the construction of a new block within the campus to connect to the Parson's Building extension (page 234). The acutely angled junction between these two straight blocks is achieved with two overlapping curved blades of façade which pivot around a tall, circular glass-block tower (looking unnervingly like the ill-fated tower to ABK's National Gallery in London, christened a 'carbuncle' by the Prince of Wales in his infamous speech). Perhaps building in a republic has encouraged its reappearance.

Internally, the accommodation is centred around an atrium, with a cascade of stairs under the large glass roof promising a fine new interior. The large floor plate of the new block is filled with partitioned-off cubicles to allow the student dentists to practise their skills on the visiting public.

ADDRESS Lincoln Place, Dublin 2
STRUCTURAL ENGINEER Ove Arup and Partners
COST IR£6.5 million
DART Pearse Station
ACCESS by appointment

Trinity College

**Ahrends Burton and Koralek 1996–**

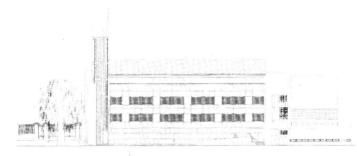

**Trinity College**

**Ahrends Burton and Koralek 1996–**

# Trinity College Library Shop

The Long Room of Trinity Library is one of the great internal spaces of Ireland; it contains a fine collection of illuminated medieval manuscripts, including the *Book of Kells*, one of Dublin's main tourist attractions. For the thousand people a day who come to view these gems, the journey begins and ends in the shop – originally an open loggia, but enclosed in the 1890s. A few years ago the space was revamped by Arthur Gibney & Partners with a new entrance lobby, external steps and ramps, and a stair down from the Long Room.

More recently, Kearney and Kiernan Architects have redesigned the shop. The architects aimed to provide clear circulation and improved selling space while acknowledging and retaining the shop's main elements. But they were also keen that commerce should not be allowed to swamp the structural and spatial qualities of the old building.

To display the merchandise, a family of related units was developed, each with a different role but connected by material and form. Together, they are capable of carrying 1800 different items. These units, dispersed within the space, respect its existing structure and circulation patterns yet develop a low-key character of their own. In this way, despite functional variety, an overall unity is achieved. Particularly successful are the window displays which manage to combine clear selling space without obscuring the view.

**Trinity College**

ADDRESS Old Library, Trinity College, Dublin 2
COST IR£150,000
BUS/TRAIN City Centre
ACCESS open

**Kearney and Kiernan Architects 1995**

SALES POINT

**Kearney and Kiernan Architects 1995**

# South Dublin

# The Sweepstakes Centre

This slick, commercial exercise is by the architect of Bolton Street College of Technology (page 70) and the Collin's Barracks (page 74). Designed to a modernist agenda, the positioning of the block on the site is governed more by practical matters – orientation, views to the Wicklow Mountains, and an internal requirement for corner offices – than by a concern for the urban block and street frontages. The location of the site, at the edge of the urban centre as it begins to break down into the suburban south, was another influential factor. These considerations have led to a 45-degree plan rotation which gives the building a certain aloofness towards its context, a detachment compounded by heavy planting and security railings.

The building is connected to Merrion Road by a two-storey block, only recently completed (as a car showroom, by Campbell Conroy Hickey Architects) after being left unfinished for years. A layout of four similar blocks had been intended, but so far only this one has been constructed. It is raised on a plinth to avoid a local flooding risk, and this has allowed parking below. A 'u' of 13.5-metre-deep office space surrounds a central atrium, all planned as a speculative 'shell and core' development, but of a superior quality. The exterior cladding of granite and mirror glass is crisply executed (the faceted building form helping to break down the scale), and owes much to contemporary blocks in the City of London.

ADDRESS Merrion Road, Ballsbridge, Dublin 4
CLIENT Ryde Development Ireland Ltd
STRUCTURAL ENGINEER Ove Arup and Partners
COST IR£5 million
BUS 5, 7, 7A, 7X, 8, 63, 84; DART Lansdowne Road
ACCESS none

South Dublin

**Gilroy McMahon Architects 1991**

**South Dublin**

**Gilroy McMahon Architects 1991**

# British Embassy

The building of a new British Embassy in post-imperial Ireland is a significant event – and one which demands a significant building. Allies and Morrison were selected as architects after winning an invited competition in 1991. They are well known in the UK (where they have become in many ways the acceptable face of modernism) for a series of carefully considered contextual buildings which combine the International Style with earlier exemplars, particularly turn-of-the-century English 'Arts and Crafts' buildings.

The archetype chosen here is the country house, a large villa of formal design placed centrally on the site with an entrance gatehouse on the street. which introduces the style and material of the main house. A 'stable block' of lesser scale and material wraps around the rear of the villa to form courtyards and staff entrances. The main building has a formal eight-bay flat frontage of Wicklow granite with aluminium and steel details, divided horizontally into base, *piano nobile* and attic storey. The elevation is an arrangement of symmetrical elements within an asymmetrical whole. The entrance to the embassy is placed centrally within the five bays to the left, and the symmetry of the layout is emphasised by the coat-of-arms over the porch recess and a chimney at roof level. The consular entrance is more informally placed within the remaining three bays, but positioned on the approach axis from the main gate. Entry is over a bridge across a reflecting pool containing a sculpture by Susannah Heron within an assemblage of planar elements from the Ben Nicholson/Geoffrey Jellicoe stable of modernism.

Beneath its skin the building is a reinforced-concrete shell, with openings reduced to a minimum in the interests of security – in effect, the architects' main task, externally, was to clothe a 'bunker'. The principal architectural device adopted was to layer the elevations, thereby creating

**Allies and Morrison 1995**

**Allies and Morrison 1995**

the effect that the façade is a sandwich of different materials, which reveal themselves at openings and edges – an approach popularised by recent analysis of Carlo Scarpa's Castelvecchio Museum in Verona. The Italian master, however, wished to make explicit the historical layering of the old building over time, with his own interventions seen as yet another layer. Here, where the building is all new, the device is a way of decorating and, indeed, disguising the structure. The openings in the façade are made to appear larger by 'exposing' a metal layer below the granite, and the thin-veneer nature of the granite is expressed with a grillage of aluminium rails which divide up the surfaces. The roof, too, continues the theme: planes of slate slide across metal surfaces and the ridge is capped by the architects' enigmatic trademark, a ridge pole.

Internally, the theme of veneering over the structure is continued, this time with hardwood panelling and plasterboard. The overall effect is refined, even delicate – a remarkable feat considering the massively indelicate concrete shell behind. The suppression of structure, however, gives the building an insubstantial, brittle quality. Consequently it lacks the *gravitas* a more structurally expressive solution might have achieved.

ADDRESS 31 Merrion Road, Ballsbridge, Dublin 4
CLIENT The British Embassy
STRUCTURAL ENGINEER Whitby and Bird
COST IR£6.3 million
BUS 5, 7, 7A, 7X, 8, 18, 46, 84; DART Lansdowne Road
ACCESS public areas, for consular business

**Allies and Morrison 1995**

**South Dublin**

**Allies and Morrison 1995**

**Mews Houses**

A tight little conversion of two mews houses facing on to Herbert Park for a businessman and an artist. One of the buildings and plots is wider than the other – and in the inevitable triumph of commerce over culture, it belongs to the businessman. Both buildings were restored and each had a new pavilion extension constructed in the garden – one a cube, the other a linear top-lit studio. Narrow corridors connect them back to the houses.

From the street a matched pair of new openings below curved balconies faces the park. The desire to hand the symmetrical openings has been resisted, adding a small twist to the composition. The material treatment of the front door and the garage doors is the same, but a subtly placed off-centre column marks the pedestrian route. The column continues beyond the balcony up to the eaves, forming one of the favoured motifs of the rationalist group, and now to be seen on every second development across Dublin.

**South Dublin**

ADDRESS Clyde Lane, Ballsbridge, Dublin 4
CLIENT Boland and Associates
STRUCTURAL ENGINEER Roughan and O'Donovan Engineers
BUS 5, 7, 7A, 8, 18, 45 from central Busaras; DART Lansdowne Road
COST IR£165,000
ACCESS none

**Grafton Architects 1992**

**Grafton Architects 1992**

# Lecture Hall and Library, Institute of Structural Engineers

This simple two-storey brick building with a pitched roof was constructed as a mews development to the rear of a large Victorian house. The lecture hall is arranged as a *piano nobile*, with the archive below and a glazed link back to the main building. The elevations are carefully proportioned and detailed, but the main point of interest lies in the architects' attempt to suggest historical layering by building in odd fragments of construction as if from earlier buildings on the site. McCullough and Mulvin obviously had in mind the picturesque effect created by buildings on and around Roman ruins, as seen in Spain or Italy. The idea is not new: Victorian country-house architects such as George Devey used the technique, often very convincingly, to fake ageing by suggesting different phases of construction, such as an 'earlier' stone cottage embedded in a larger brick house. Here, however, ageing has not been the architects' intention because the 'older' fragments – the arch over the circular window to the rear elevation and the exposed brick arches in the plastered wall of the stairwell – are clearly contemporary with the rest. Perhaps only the 'idea' of historical layering was important. Whatever was intended, it was guaranteed to drive old modernists to apoplexy, and the architects have not, to our knowledge, tried the experiment again.

ADDRESS 22 Clyde Road, Ballsbridge, Dublin 4
CLIENT Institute of Engineers of Ireland
STRUCTURAL ENGINEER Joseph McCullough and Partners
COST IR£400,000
BUS 5, 7, 7A, 8, 18, 45; DART Lansdowne Road
ACCESS none

**South Dublin**

**McCullough and Mulvin Architects 1989**

# House

With modern houses such a rarity in suburban Dublin, the arrival of this small International Style villa is a cause for celebration. It was constructed for a retired couple in the grounds of their larger house, on a site without a rear aspect. A shallow curved wall defines this south-east boundary, and a single bank of accommodation faces west to the garden and road. Utilising the existing features of the site, particularly some substantial garden walls, the architects conceived the plan as a sequence of layers.

Entry from the street is into an outer garden, a space between two of the retained walls. The inner wall is breached by a new grouping of crisp white railings and a Scarpa-like fountain indicating entry. A pivoting gate leads to the inner garden, where water cascades line the route to the front door. The front of the house is formalised with a free-standing concrete arcade screen. The wall of the house behind is heavily planted and will eventually appear as a green backdrop (punctuated by windows and glass-block panels) to the white screen wall and the water garden. Projecting horizontal canopies define the position of the front door and living-room terrace. The section of the house has been carefully manipulated to allow maximum sun and light penetration – so the masses can perform their 'masterly, correct and magnificent play'.

ADDRESS 40A Anglesea Road, Ballsbridge, Dublin 4
CLIENT Mr and Mrs J Dolan
STRUCTURAL ENGINEER Clifton Scannell Emerson Associates
COST IR£250,000
BUS 46, 63, 84 from city centre
ACCESS none

South Dublin

**Noel Dowley Architects 1995**

**South Dublin**

**Noel Dowley Architects 1995**

# Swan Place Housing Development

This early, possibly the first, housing scheme from the rationalist group – built at the end of a narrow mews on a small land-locked site – remains a skilful and relevant solution to the problem of dense inner-city housing. To form a row of three houses, the site is divided into six parallel strips with each house having one two-storey block and a second which is split between courtyards at the rear and bedrooms to the front, connected by a glass wall. At first-floor level over the bedrooms are glass-roofed conservatories. From the mews these are expressed as a series of alternately solid or glazed gables.

At street level an arcade provides the formal street frontage and creates a buffer zone. It also leads to the parking spaces, which are accessed from another road. Front doors open off the arcade; circular columns within the mostly square arcade piers subtly indicate their location.

Nothing needs to be added or taken away from this development: it provides private, sunny homes with a variety of living spaces, achieved with an admirable economy of means.

ADDRESS Swan Place, off Leeson Street Upper/The Appian Way, Ranelagh, Dublin 4
CLIENT Ray Doyle Construction
COST IR£100,000
BUS 10, 11, 11A, 11B, 13, 18, 46A, 46B; DART Lansdowne Road
ACCESS none

**South Dublin**

**Shay Cleary and Frank Hall 1983**

**Shay Cleary and Frank Hall 1983**

# Beggars Bush Barracks Housing Development

Private housing developments have been the mainstay of the Dublin construction industry for decades, and the southern suburbs in particular have seen massive new schemes. But finding architectural merit amongst them is akin to finding the proverbial needle in the haystack. This densely packed scheme is almost alone in transcending populist boundaries in search of a more urban form.

Beyond the gateway into Haddington Square, the original barracks buildings remain to the sides and a large government laboratory block dominates the view ahead. The new housing is disposed behind the original terraces in parallel blocks, with one block laminated on to the rear of the original buildings. The spaces between the blocks alternate between gardens and entrance courts. At the end of the terraces a row of single-storey houses follows the line of Haddington Road.

The palette of materials is austere – brick and grey metal for windows and railings, with some glass block to the garden side. Interest comes from bay rhythms, the tall Dutch proportion of openings, and the occasional dishing or curving articulation to the brick forms. The entrance courtyards are signalled by a cutaway corner with full-height corner columns.

ADDRESS Haddington Square, Haddington Road, Dublin 4
CLIENT Gem Development Company Ltd
COST IR£5 million
STRUCTURAL ENGINEER Thorburn Colquhoun
BUS 45; DART Lansdowne Road
ACCESS none

**South Dublin**

**Shay Cleary Architects 1995**

**The Islamic Cultural Centre**

The centre, discreetly set back from the road in deepest south suburbia, is one of the most unexpected new buildings in Dublin. In keeping with the all-encompassing nature of the Islamic faith, it comprises a complex mix of uses, making the centre a village in microcosm. As well as the central prayer hall there is a school, sports hall, shop, restaurant, library, meeting and training rooms, and ten apartments. Such a diverse mix is made possible by the plan: a deceptively simple and apposite tartan grid which demonstrates a satisfying level of resolution achieved only by exhaustive study and refinement.

The prayer hall is surrounded by a 360-degree ambulatory, and this feature, together with a family entrance, marks the building as innovatory within the Islamic world. Aside from the emblematic dome and minaret, a distinct Islamic character has been achieved without recourse to detail pastiche. All decorative elements, from balustrading and window tracery to rooflights and marble tiling, relate back to the square-plan diagram. However, the building's obligatory orientation towards Mecca creates a rather indeterminate relationship with the street and site, although it satisfies the client's desire not to appear dominant within the local scene. The minaret, incidentally, is symbolic – south Dublin will not be serenaded with calls to prayer at regular intervals during the day.

ADDRESS adjacent to Rosemount Crescent, Roebuck Road, Clonskeagh, Dublin
CLIENT The Islamic Foundation of Ireland
STRUCTURAL ENGINEER Ove Arup and Partners
BUS 11, 11A, 11B, 62
ACCESS none

**Michael Collins and Associates 1996**

South Dublin

**South Dublin**

**Michael Collins and Associates 1996**

# Dun Laoghaire Harbour Ferry Terminal

Dun Laoghaire, the country's busiest ferry terminal, is for many people their first sight of Ireland. The arrival of the futuristic HSS ferry, a catamaran the size of a football pitch, has prompted a reorganisation of the whole area and the construction of a new terminal building.

Planned to provide an experience associated more with airports than traditional seaports, the new building has arrivals and departure lounges and baggage handling and reclaim areas. It takes the form of a long, thin flow diagram connecting the ferry to land. From where the HSS berths at the far end, foot passengers cross a 'linkspan' bridge to the new terminal – cars disembark in the normal manner to the side of the building. The arrivals hall is on the top deck beneath the shallow curved roof. From here, a series of escalators and stairs take passengers down to the ground-floor baggage reclaim and then to the arrivals hall and out into the town. Departing passengers follow the reverse route to the departure lounges, on a different floor.

Externally the arrivals/departures split is articulated by a large granite-clad fin wall projecting out from the bow of the centrally placed multideck lounge. Crowning this is a steel and glass rotunda which provides a central focus as the building fans out around it in an unruly collection of curves, angles and facets. The construction and materials – white cladding panels with a superstructure of lightweight steel stairs and balconies – continue the nautical theme and give the terminal itself, particularly the projecting lounge section, the appearance of a docked ferry.

The building is connected to the town by an audacious new landscaped plaza, seemingly transplanted whole from Barcelona complete with palm trees and flagpoles arranged in matching geometric groups and Gaudí-style serpentine seating faced in irregular, coloured mosaics. In the main plaza area on the departures side of the fin wall, a line of elegant lights

**Burke-Kennedy Doyle and Partners 1995**

**Burke-Kennedy Doyle and Partners 1995**

leads to the entrance. The perimeter of the plaza is neatly defined by a wall which allows a distant view of the sea and Howth Head while editing out the foreground paraphernalia of the dockside. The wall sweeps around to enclose the space and its tableau of streetscape objects, including Gaoth Na Saile (Salt Wind), a new sculpture by Eamonn O'Doherty (see page 40), and a water fountain. The whole ensemble speaks of travel and foreign parts, and uses quotations in a manner similar to Hans Hollein's famous travel agencies.

The decision to influence visitors' first impressions of Ireland with such an outward-looking European-influenced design is indicative of the current positive and self-confident mood of the country.

ADDRESS Dun Laoghaire Port, Harbour Road, Dun Laoghaire, Co. Dublin
CLIENT Department of the Marine
LANDSCAPE ARCHITECT Mitchell Associates
STRUCTURAL ENGINEER P H McCarthy and Partners
COST IR£16 million
BUS 45A, 45B, 46A, 59, 75, 111; DART Dun Laoghaire
ACCESS open

**South Dublin**

**Burke-Kennedy Doyle and Partners 1995**

**South Dublin**

**Burke-Kennedy Doyle and Partners 1995**

# Civic Offices, Dun Laoghaire

Recent reorganisation of Dublin's local-government boundaries has lead to a series of new county halls – in Tallaght (see page 290), in central Dublin, here at Dun Laoghaire, and in Swords, north Dublin, where the Fingal County Hall is under construction to designs by Bucholz McEvoy and BDP. The Dun Laoghaire-Rathdown Civic Offices are an extension to the original polychromatic town hall (1860), which is also the centrepiece of a fine group of high-Victorian public buildings including the railway station and adjacent yacht clubs. The new building is very much a contextual extension with no ambition to dominate the older building despite the fact that it is, at 10,000 square metres, more than four times as large. The principal new elevation to Crofton Road dutifully matches the materials and all the main horizontal lines of its mentor but with no attempt at detail replication. Instead, the architects have developed a cool, restrained modernism which achieves a skilful balance between old and new, similar to, for example, Gunnar Asplund's Gothenburg law courts project. Also like that modern classic is the doughnut plan revolving around a three-storey atrium lit, in this case, by a bank of vaulted monitor rooflights. The intended flexibility of the central space for meetings, exhibitions and recitals, and as 'the interface between the public and the local authority', is achieved with large-scale folding and sliding partitions. The servicing of the building follows a 'green' agenda of natural ventilation with stack-effect ventilation towers breaking the roofline, an enlightened policy promoted in all Dublin's new town halls.

ADDRESS corner of Crofton Road and Royal Marine Road, Dun Laoghaire, Co. Dublin
COST IR£8.5 million
BUS 8, 45A, 45B, 46A, 59, 75, 111; DART Dun Laoghaire
ACCESS open

South Dublin

**McCullough and Mulvin Architects/ Robinson Keefe and Devane 1996**

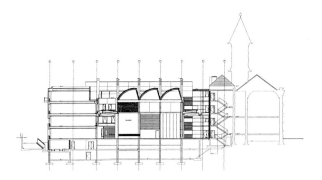

**McCullough and Mulvin Architects/ Robinson Keefe and Devane**

**Fire Station**

A good example of a modern continuation of the 'Functional Tradition', this fire station is planned on a consistent ten-bay structural module with exposed blockwork cross-walls and a tidy, steel-truss roof structure. Into this utilitarian framework are slotted the various elements of the brief – from the fire appliance garage to facilities for 100 staff (including mess and muster areas, and dormitories and offices surrounding a landscaped courtyard).

To the street the end bays are filled with masonry panels, but to the rear the building opens up with lightweight infill sections overlooking the courtyard – apart from the garage, which is glazed on both sides to give views of the red appliances within. The overall result has been achieved, without self-conscious architectonic devices, by simply following the logic of the original well-conceived strategic decisions. Refreshing.

ADDRESS Kill Avenue, Dun Laoghaire, Co. Dublin
CLIENT Dun Laoghaire Corporation
ARCHITECT IN CHARGE Edward Conroy
STRUCTURAL ENGINEER Michael Punch and Partners
COST IR£2.24 million
BUS 46A; DART Dun Laoghaire
ACCESS none

**South Dublin**

**Dun Laoghaire Architects Department 1991**

**South Dublin**

**Dun Laoghaire Architects Department 1991**

# University College Dublin, School of Engineering

Scott Tallon Walker have had an extraordinary run of plum commissions for the major educational establishments in Ireland, most notably the masterplan for Galway University, a series of buildings at Trinity College, and here at University College Dublin (UCD). Their recent projects (mostly covered in this book) form a consistent body of work in which they reinterpret a limited collection of forms and ideas in diverse building types. In particular, STW are interested in the creation of modular, extendible strategies and construction. The largest within this group of work is the School of Engineering, commissioned in 1974 with phase 1 completed in 1989, comprising 13,000 square metres of space. With its collection of workshops, foundries and laboratories, it is large in scale and heavyweight in use.

The building is currently cast adrift on the UCD campus, awaiting phase 2 to connect it to the main east–west spine. The glazed concourse is set out on the axis of the earlier STW Industries Centre (page 272), with which it shares a common language, or *the* common language since both buildings resemble all the others, both here and at Trinity. The glazed concourse, on four floors, generates the plan, and four wings are planned to plug into the concourse from the west. So far only two wings have been built. Nestling between them is a single-storey workshop roofed by a steel suspension structure. Further accommodation, mainly small offices, occupies short wings to the east of the concourse.

The main entrance, signalled by projecting glazed bays, is for no obvious reason raised up to first-floor level, hence the large stair open to the elements. This move was apparently in response to the client's request for a 'walk-up building', but it gives the building an aloofness from its surroundings, exacerbated by the surrounding Tarmac moat and concrete

**Scott Tallon Walker Architects 1989**

**Scott Tallon Walker Architects 1989**

walls. Apart from the entrance bay (to be replicated at the other end of the concourse when phase 2 is completed), the building is entirely wrapped up in a cladding system of square granite-aggregate GRC panels, with matching square windows or louvre panels. Some incident is achieved by the blank, concrete stair towers at the ends of each wing, but overall the building is opaque, with virtually no views into the interiors. Interesting features inside include an early beam engine moved here from the Guinness Brewery, and an open, steel lift structure.

Although on a much larger scale, the design here is reminiscent of Nicholas Grimshaw's early 'high-tech' warehouses, where the main interest was in the cladding system, in the intellectual game of satisfying the many different elevational conditions with as few interchangeable panel types as possible. Reflecting on how Grimshaw might resolve this problem today, however, one thinks instead of a building such as the Financial Times Printworks, where glass walls on to the workshops display the use of the building and animate the space around it.

The School of Engineering clearly solves the organisational and constructional aspects of a complex brief, with rigorous integration of structure and services matched by a high level of detailed resolution, but it offers little to the exterior life of the campus.

ADDRESS University College Dublin, Belfield, Dublin 4
STRUCTURAL ENGINEER Ove Arup and Partners
COST IR£13 million
BUS 3, 10, 11B, 17, 52
ACCESS none

**South Dublin**

**Scott Tallon Walker Architects 1989**

**South Dublin**

**Scott Tallon Walker Architects 1989**

# University Industries Centre, University College Dublin

The Industries Centre, the first example of the granite-aggregate GRC wall-cladding system familiar to most of the architects' recent buildings, was conceived as a forum of interaction between engineering students and industry at large. This relationship is made explicit by siting the building close to, and axially connected to, the entrance and concourse of the adjacent School of Engineering (see page 268).

The single-volume building has a raked-seating auditorium, connected at its highest level to an exhibition area. Its unusual triangular plan, derived from the fan shape of the 250-seat auditorium, lends a monumentality which allows this small building to make its mark within the wide open campus spaces. The geometry of the plan is reflected in the triangulated roof structure, and the same grid controls all the internal walls and spaces.

Behind the building, the entrance kiosk to the university, a jewel-like structure, also by Scott Tallon Walker Architects, is worth a look. Note how an almost neolithic chunk of concrete is played off against a delicate frameless glass box sheltering below.

**South Dublin**

ADDRESS University College Dublin, Belfield, Dublin 4
STRUCTURAL ENGINEER Ove Arup and Partners
COST IR£1 million
BUS 3, 10, 11B, 17, 52
ACCESS none

**Scott Tallon Walker Architects 1985**

**South Dublin**

**Scott Tallon Walker Architects 1985**

# O'Reilly Hall, University College Dublin

The new hall, at the northern end of the central circulation spine, has a simple plan with a large rectangular auditorium entered end-on beneath a freestanding portal. On the lakeside is a large-scale eight-bay loggia, with the fully glazed walls set back to form a covered external arcade.

The hall continues the Miesian tradition of the halcyon days when STW were producing buildings such as the Bank of Ireland headquarters. The purity of Mies van der Rohe's vision remains a driving force, but his structural clarity has been subsumed by an overriding interest in the skin. Although the resolution of the hall's cladding system is admirable, cladding the arcade columns to match the walls displays a lack of interest in the tectonic that Mies himself would never have shown.

The geometry of the square is everywhere, from the cube of the entrance portal, to the arcade proportions, to the cladding-panel grid. Mies, however, was not greatly interested in the square, possibly recognising a danger of banality in its easy abstraction. STW's use of the same cladding system on virtually all their recent buildings is in itself a remarkable feat of consistency. Perhaps they follow the view (practised by Tadao Ando) that predetermining materials frees the architect to concentrate on more fundamental issues. Or perhaps it is the unrepentant modernist's way of avoiding the fashionable or ephemeral. But it is hard to avoid a sense of *déjà vu* when faced with yet another GRC grid.

ADDRESS University College Dublin, Belfield, Dublin 4
STRUCTURAL ENGINEERS Keogh and McConnell/Ove Arup and Partners
COST IR£3.1 million
BUS 3, 10, 11B, 17, 52
ACCESS none

**South Dublin**

**Scott Tallon Walker Architects 1994**

**Scott Tallon Walker Architects 1994**

# Biotechnology Research Building, University College Dublin

A small research laboratory building displaying the trademark Scott Tallon Walker palette of materials and details – square GRC panels and flush aluminium windows – is here given a twist in the form of a large curved bay and curved glass-block stair towers. It is essentially a simple rectangular block of laboratories on two storeys, with a central corridor connecting the towers. The curved bay provides the research chemists with workstations separate from the labs. The curve also marks the entrance location, indicated more clearly by the approach steps and path than by any clues on the elevation, where the doors are not allowed to break the square grid.

Internally, the reception desk marks the centre of a semi-circle with a mural backdrop. Upstairs, a rooflight at the centre point illuminates a central meeting room within the open-plan workstation area, designed to encourage interaction between the boffins.

Externally, the building's character is formed by a wide aluminium *brise-soleil* whose circular fixing points for the suspension wires form a pattern around the curve. As always with STW, the building gains an extra dimension from the precision and quality of the construction and the clarity of the plan diagram.

ADDRESS University College Dublin, Belfield, Dublin 4
STRUCTURAL ENGINEER Ove Arup and Partners
BUS 3, 10, 11B, 17, 52
ACCESS none

**Scott Tallon Walker Architects 1994**

**Scott Tallon Walker Architects 1994**

# Deans of Residence Chaplaincy

The brief called for residential units for five priests, along with communal facilities, a large meeting room and a contemplation room. The model followed is the country house, with a symmetrical disposition of rooms reflected in formal elevations. The house is split horizontally into two double-height layers, an unusually sectional arrangement of spaces only hinted at in the elevations. The entrance hall leads axially to the central meeting room, which has a shallow curved bay to the garden front. To the sides of the meeting room are mezzanines containing the kitchens, housekeeper's flat and utility spaces. A projecting drum to the side of the main block houses the contemplation room. The upper level consists of a row of five residential units, arranged as double-height living areas facing the garden and bedroom mezzanines and balconies overlooking the living area.

The country-house precedent is explicit in the starkly symmetrical elevations. The entrance front, opposite the huge School of Engineering (page 268) with which it has an axial relationship, follows tradition and is the more formal and closed elevation, while the south-facing garden front with its curved bay and larger windows is more open. Both elevations make a cool, rational and controlled statement from a former student and employee of Mies van der Rohe, and professor of architecture at UCD from 1973 to 1995.

ADDRESS University College Dublin, Belfield, Dublin 4
STRUCTURAL ENGINEER Joseph McCullough and Partners
BUS 3, 10, 11B, 17, 52
ACCESS none

**South Dublin**

**Professor Cathal O'Neill and Partners 1989**

**South Dublin**

**Professor Cathal O'Neill and Partners 1989**

**Drive-In Bank**

This first drive-in bank in Europe forms a distinctive landmark on the main road into Dublin from the south, particularly at night when the glowing roof hovers above the ground like a visiting UFO. It is also a symbol of the suburbanisation of Dublin, offering the 'convenience' of a visit to the bank without leaving the protective cocoon of your car.

The main building, with its roof suspended from a central concrete core, is in fact a regular bank, with the drive-in elements arranged as separate automatic teller machines. Vehicle circulation has both governed the site layout and generated the circular form of the main bank. The elaborate steel structure gives the impression of being a cantilever off the central core, but in fact it supports the external canopy edge which springs from a ring beam over the external walls.

ADDRESS Cornelscourt, Co. Dublin
CLIENT Allied Irish Bank
STRUCTURAL ENGINEER Horgan Lynch and Partners
BUS 45, 46, 84, 86
ACCESS drive-in facilities open 24 hours

**Robinson Keefe and Devane 1990**

**South Dublin**

**Robinson Keefe and Devane 1990**

# Charlesland Golf Club and Hotel

Greystones lies right on the edge of the Dublin conurbation, in a location that is becoming steadily more accessible to the centre as road and rail links are improved. What was once a holiday location for Dubliners is now commuter territory, and with the changing demography has come the requirement for leisure pursuits, particularly golf. Charlesland is a new golf links, with clubhouse and a small hotel attached. The club and hotel sit in idyllic rolling countryside between the sea and the Wicklow Mountains, at the centre of the new course. The accommodation is split into two linear blocks: the one to the south contains the principal function rooms – bar, banqueting and dining rooms – and that to the north the bedrooms, offices and service areas. The northern range is canted at an angle to form a tapering top-lit central hall between the blocks to provide the main circulation areas.

Paul Keogh's early reputation was based on a series of small projects which found a way of combining traditional, often classically based, forms and details into contemporary projects – a theme which is continued here, especially in the interior fittings. The building sits low in the landscape, with the two linear blocks roofed with monopitches. An elliptical entrance court leads to the entrance, positioned at the end of the central mall. Along the south façade three conservatory bays rise above the eaves line to capture sun and view. The main rooms are expressed as white, rendered blocks, while a flat-roofed red-brick strip running through the design contains the service areas. The balance of forms is clearly modern, but refers also to more traditional roots – seaside buildings in particular.

Internally the central mall is enlivened by changing levels. The formal suite of rooms to the south announces itself within the space by a range of sculptural openings along their north wall, and the lounge at the end

**Paul Keogh Architects 1992**

**Paul Keogh Architects 1992**

of the mall is formed most distinctively by a semi-circular extrusion through the depth of the services strip. The interiors are characterised by symmetrical groupings of sculptural elements with traditionally based but recognisably contemporary detailing, much of it in beech. The spirit of Edwardian arts and crafts infuses the interior, and fittings such as fire places and wall panelling are reminiscent of, say, the Mary Ward Settlement in London, or below-stairs in country houses. The bays to the south allow circulation between the function rooms and provide access to the terrace, from where there are views of the final hole.

The plan of the upper areas is a model of resolution and clarity, as is the connection of the south-facing function rooms, via the bays, to the terrace and the course beyond. It has been achieved at a price, however; locker rooms, changing areas and the sauna/plunge pools have been demoted to basement areas, without light or view. None the less, the building remains an important indication that tradition and precedent can be skilfully combined to produce sophisticated buildings that can engage with context and the contemporary world.

ADDRESS Charlesland Golf Club, Greystones, Co. Wicklow
CLIENT Charlesland Golf and Sporting Services Ltd
STRUCTURAL ENGINEER John Moylan and Associates
COST IR£2 million
DART Greystones
ACCESS hotel open to the public

**South Dublin**

**Paul Keogh Architects 1992**

**Paul Keogh Architects 1992**

# West Dublin

**'The Square' Shopping Centre**

Tallaght is new-town Dublin. Begun in the early 1970s when Dublin was the fastest growing capital in Europe, it is now the fourth largest town in Ireland, made from mile upon soul-crushing mile of identical semis. The car is an essential aid to survival here, and all roads inevitably lead to 'The Square', whose great pyramid roof looms over the surrounding approach roads like a pharaoh of commerce beckoning the faithful.

Park in the 2000-car space encircling the temple and enter the Brave New World – if you can find an entrance. This behemoth may have around 55,700 square metres of shopping but it has only four entrances. Its blank elevations show that this building is not concerned with the city or shaping urban space; it is about creating a fantasy world where the sun always shines, the palm trees sway in the breeze, and you can forget that Tallaght exists. The imagery may, however, prompt a different daydream. Maybe this *is* Aldous Huxley's future, an internal refuge against a poisoned world. Maybe the chaotic and dizzying maze of malls exists because there is no exit. Maybe an electric waterfall and potted trees are all that remain of nature; and the stale air, stuffy heat and claustrophobic press of the crowd mean there are more people here than the system can support … Paranoia aside, the mall-based internal shopping centre is no doubt here to stay, and this is Dublin's largest example – at least until nearby Blanchardstown is finished.

ADDRESS Tallaght Town Centre, Blessington Road, Dublin 24
CLIENT Monarch Properties Ltd and GRE Properties Ltd
STRUCTURAL ENGINEER T J O'Connor and Associates
COST IR£40 million
BUS 49, 54A, 56A, 75, 201, 203
ACCESS open

**West Dublin**

**Burke-Kennedy Doyle and Partners 1990**

**West Dublin**

**Burke-Kennedy Doyle and Partners 1990**

**South Dublin Civic Offices**

The north exit from 'The Square' (page 288) leads to a pedestrian axis to the new South Dublin Civic Centre, whose civic role is indicated by a rising monopitch and beacon. On approach, any doubt as to the position of the entrance is lost when the low building to your left is passed and the path widens out into an entrance courtyard. You are immediately transported from Tallaght to Scandinavia. Soft brown brick, Louis Poulson lights and pantile roofs swooping down close to the ground strike that delicate balance between civic stature and friendly, approachable domesticity encountered in the best Danish work. The finishing touch to the space is an apposite stainless-steel sculpture by Mike Bulfin symbolising 'the community'.

The main entrance doors open into a top-lit east–west orientated public concourse which soars up three storeys to a delicate steel-trussed roof and forms the main public areas. The second public entrance is into the concourse from the east, where it relates to a perceived axial relationship with the Regional Technical College (see page 294) half a mile to the east. An important aspect of the planning was a desire to carve an urban relationship between the main buildings of Tallaght, out of the surrounding and unyielding dross. This formal structure will grow, one hopes, as other public buildings – a new transport interchange, for example – are built.

The concourse houses the departmental counters and a café, and entered off it are the library and the council chamber complex to the south. Behind to the north lie the main office areas. The council chamber itself is elegantly underplayed, with a simple but expressive 'forum-in-the-round' layout. A corner window opens directly on to the entrance courtyard, giving passers-by a view of their elected representatives in action – a brave gesture towards 'transparent democracy'. When we were

**Gilroy McMahon Architects 1994**

**Gilroy McMahon Architects 1994**

visiting this had already been obscured by a curtain, but whether this was to shield the sun or the democracy was not explained.

The building was constructed under a 'design and build' procedure, new to Ireland but common elsewhere in Europe, where the building contractor controls the total works and makes the architect his subcontractor. This makes cost control at least as important as the architecture (and usually more so) and requires flexibility of approach on the part of the architect. Des McMahon suggests that in these instances the architect has to 'pick his targets' and concentrate on certain areas at the expense of others. At the civic offices the public spaces were the target, and the quality is very high. Touches such as the ceramic wall lining at low level give a crisp finish with a Scandinavian touch and will wear and age well. The office areas to the north, though, give the impression that the builder was more in control here, and are mundane by comparison. Taken overall, however, this is a building to give Tallaght hope.

ADDRESS Tallaght Town Centre, Blessington Road, Tallaght, Dublin 24
CLIENT South Dublin Civic Council
STRUCTURAL ENGINEER T J O'Connor and Associates
COST IR£8 million
BUS 49, 54A, 56A, 75, 201, 203
ACCESS open

**Gilroy McMahon Architects 1994**

**Gilroy McMahon Architects 1994**

# Regional Technical College

This is an old-fashioned building, and none the worse for that. At a time when the architectural debate is so style-centred it is refreshing to see a new building which looks back to the modernist ideals of solving problems by rational analysis, and developing an architectural system that integrates the structure, circulation, services installations and use-patterns into a clear and logical whole.

The college is a tertiary-level establishment with a full range of campus facilities catering for 1000 students in three separate departments – Business, Engineering, and Science. Entry from the east passes the library where the views of students at work set an appropriate tone. The entrance hall rises the full three storeys of the building, with all the principal social spaces – the dining hall, library and main lecture hall – gathered around it. The combination of the triple-height entrance hall and the adjacent double-height dining room (with a huge south-facing glazed wall) makes a dramatic entrance sequence, embellished with modernist touches such as circular rooflights and a curving, grand-piano-shaped balcony.

The key to the organisation is the spine or internal street on to which the varied accommodation is plugged where required. The spine also caters for the main service routes, circulation and fire escape, and makes future expansion a simple matter. The entrance hall plugs directly on to the spine, which then sets off in a northerly direction, laying out the lecture rooms, laboratories and other accommodation as it goes. The blocks to the west are separated by courtyards containing stairs off the spine, colour-coded for identification. The library courtyard is already fully enclosed; phase 2 will complete the enclosure of the other two courtyards with a new block parallel to the spine.

Externally, rather than being self-consciously composed, the elevations are developed directly from the plan and section and from the needs of

**West Dublin**

**Brady Shipman Martin 1992**

**Brady Shipman Martin 1992**

orientation. Materials are consistent and from a limited palette – for the most part, exposed blocks and aluminium windows.

Internally, most materials are left exposed, in particular the beefy concrete frame and block walls. Only the use of a suspended ceiling strikes a jarring note – exposed services would have added a further level of clarity and extended the sense of 'materiality' displayed elsewhere. It is all very straightforward and free from artifice.

ADDRESS Blessington Road, Tallaght, Dublin 24
CLIENT Department of Education
STRUCTURAL ENGINEER James Harrington Associates
COST IR£8 million
BUS 49, 49A, 50A, 54, 56A, 65, 65A, 65B, 77, 77A, 77B from city centre
ACCESS by appointment

**West Dublin**

**Brady Shipman Martin 1992**

**Brady Shipman Martin 1992**

# Firhouse Parish Church

This is one of de Blacam and Meagher's first buildings, won in competition, and has an unusual and highly abstract character. The exterior form – an unrelieved rectangular blockwork compound – creates a secret world reminiscent of the walled gardens of country houses. Entry is indicated by a small free-standing portico at the south-west corner. In plan the compound is split into three square grids across and four down, allowing a cruciform church to be laid out with courtyards at the four corners. The church itself is a flat-roofed concrete frame on a tartan grid, arranged traditionally as a two-bay nave, crossing, chancel and transepts. Walls facing the courtyards are fully glazed and can be left open during services in summer, blurring the boundary between the interior spaces and the tree-planted courtyards. The concept of the walled garden is loaded with religious imagery, as is the concealment of its exterior, followed by the transparency and openness discovered on admittance.

The architectural imagery is no less potent, recalling the courtyard houses of Mies van der Rohe with lashings of Louis Kahn and Gunnar Asplund thrown in. The church is an object lesson in how a simple architectural idea and layout can generate such richness of meaning and interpretation.

ADDRESS Firhouse Road, Firhouse, Dublin
CLIENT Catholic Archdiocese of Dublin
STRUCTURAL ENGINEER Joseph McCullough and Partners
COST IR£150,000
BUS 49, 50, 75
ACCESS open

West Dublin

**de Blacam and Meagher Architects 1978**

**West Dublin**

**de Blacam and Meagher Architects 1978**

# Index

**Dublin: a guide to recent architecture**

Dublin: a guide to recent architecture

Dublin: a guide to recent architecture

Photographs by Keith Collie except page 123, by Kate Horgan; pages 245 and 247, by Peter Cook